THE ATLANTIC FANTASY:
THE U.S., NATO, AND EUROPE

Studies in International Affairs Number 13

Studies in International Affairs Number 13

THE ATLANTIC FANTASY: THE U.S., NATO, AND EUROPE

by David Calleo

The Washington Center of Foreign Policy Research
School of Advanced International Studies
The Johns Hopkins University

The Johns Hopkins Press, Baltimore and London

The Johns Hopkins Press, Baltimore, Maryland 21218
The Johns Hopkins Press Ltd., London

Library of Congress Catalog Card Number 75–128823

ISBN 0–8018–1222–4 (clothbound edition)
ISBN 0–8018–1196–1 (paperback edition)

To Professor Eugene V. Rostow

CONTENTS

PREFACE

For the past several years, America's role in European defense has been the subject of an intermittent and rather sluggish debate. On the whole, public discussion has been one-sided. With a few distinguished exceptions, the great bulk of expert opinion appears to favor continuing our present military role in Europe. Many oppose any reduction whatsoever in our military forces on the continent. Most who have spoken, to be sure, are men with a strong attachment to the existing institutions, like NATO, and to the strategic and political concepts that justify them. For revisionist critics, worried about an American drift toward imperialism, Vietnam has naturally seemed the central issue. But in many respects, Europe offers a more crucial test of America's long-range international predilections.

European affairs are rapidly approaching the point where it is possible and desirable for the United States to devolve the heavy responsibilities it has carried since World War II. The time is at hand not for a return to American isolationism, but for a resumption of European responsibilities. Should we attempt to prolong our postwar burdens and privileges much longer, we run the risk of unravelling that Western European and transatlantic solidarity whose fostering has been the glory of our postwar diplomacy. We cannot govern an "Atlantic community" from Washington. The attempt will fail in the end and will corrupt and embitter us both. The Europeans are our best friends in the world; they are also our equals. When all is said and done, Europe is not America's front porch, but somebody else's house.

But before there can be a shift in our policies, there must be a shift in our imaginations—away from that two-dimensional myth of blocs and challenges to a vision that represents that plural squirming world which is reality. The following may, I hope, contribute something to transforming the country's political imagination.

I have had a great deal of help in writing this book. Its initial inspiration came from a year spent as consultant to former Under Secretary of State for Political Affairs Eugene V. Rostow. It should doubtless be apparent that Mr. Rostow and I have some differing views on European affairs. It was no less apparent at the time. But Eugene Rostow is one of those admirable people strong enough to combine convictions and passions of their own with a genuine appreciation for strong-minded dissent. It is not surprising that Rostow has been one of the great deans in the history of Yale's Law School. Working for him in the State Department was an extraordinarily stimulating and agreeable experience, as well as a great lesson in the practice of academic freedom and integrity. I shall always be grateful.

A book which sweeps across so many topics needs a great deal of research. I have been helped not only by numerous kind friends in Europe and Washington, among them several of my colleagues at the Washington Center of Foreign Policy Research, but also by some excellent assistants from among my students at the School of Advanced International Studies. Both John Berger and Götz Schreiber have contributed important information and ideas at various stages. Benjamin Rowland has worked on this book from the beginning and has made a major contribution to its development. All have assisted with the chores, along with my secretary, Diane Nielsen. I could never have finished without their loyal help and forbearance.

THE ATLANTIC FANTASY:
THE U.S., NATO, AND EUROPE

Studies in International Affairs Number 13

I.
THE AMERICAN CRISIS:
NATIONAL ASPIRATIONS AND
WORLDWIDE COMMITMENTS

Future historians may be puzzled by the present-day rebirth of American "isolationism"—not because it came at all, but because it took so long in coming. How the American public, with its prewar diffidence about events abroad, could so easily accept a shift to postwar involvement everywhere will certainly invite explanation. Some historians will doubtless suggest that America's isolationism and imperialism, like many opposites, had a secret affinity.

In any event, the extent of America's transformation is breathtaking. For over twenty years, Americans have accepted the view that their country is the active leader of at least half the world and, in some special way, charged with responsibility for the whole. America's power and attention have been so drawn outward that the whole postwar international system has been long described as a Russian-American "duopoly." In what has become the standard view of the postwar system, the two superpowers—armed with nuclear arsenals, messianic ideologies, and strong governments—have each built up a large system of clients and protectorates and extended a rival presence to nearly every part of the Third World.

Whether this view of things corresponds particularly to the realities of the postwar world is, in one sense, an irrelevant question. By controlling the imaginations of statesmen, scholars, and the general public in all countries, the myth of duopoly exerts a powerful influence on the governments of America, Russia, and most everywhere else. The myth tends to make real the situation it imagines to be true, because we live increasingly in a world dominated more by art than by nature. Today's technological affluence frees powerful states from the tyranny of "stubborn facts" more than ever before, and it begins to look, after all, as if it was Marx and not Hegel who was standing on his head. If anything, ideas today determine policies more than ever before.

In any event, American policy, believing in duopoly, has worked hard to make it a reality. It is the growing strain of this effort, however, which has provoked the neoisolationist public reaction in America. In Vietnam, the "facts" have been flouted too outrageously and the myth has been challenged. American public opinion has at last begun to question the entire foundation of the country's foreign policy.

But the ideal of duopoly will not fade easily, at home or abroad. It has become institutionalized in numerous policies, arrangements, and perspectives, and to many it seems a not unreasonable way to organize the international system. Considering its unpromising roots in the Cold War, duopoly now appears to offer a rather comfortable stability. According to its contemporary version, the two competing superpowers, conscious of the nuclear balance of terror, have moved toward a seemingly durable understanding to respect each other's camp and to limit confrontations in the Third World.* In many respects, the new system can present itself as an

---

* Dean Rusk vigorously denied that any explicit arrangement exists, or that the Russians respect any tacit arrangement. "Some Myths and Misconceptions about U.S. Foreign Policy," *Department of State Bulletin*, October 7, 1968, pp. 350–56.

impressive improvement over the perilous volatility that existed before World War II. Certainly in Europe, where the two blocs are most clearly defined, both camps, under their respective nuclear umbrellas, have felt a sense of military stability uncommon in recent memory.

European stability seems all the more remarkable because it appears to defy the political laws of gravity. Twenty-five years after World War II, Germany still remains arbitrarily divided, as indeed does Europe as a whole. A continent that has for centuries formed a sort of political, economic, and cultural system is still kept apart by brutal military force. Yet this seemingly provisional arrangement has already lasted longer than the Versailles Treaty.

Many commentators are inclined to believe that the model of duopoly will define the future, that America and Russia, each presiding in its fashion over an increasingly integrated system of allies and clients, will—as Tocqueville once predicted—ultimately come to divide the world between them.[1] Or to put this another way, both superpowers, driven by an imperative common interest in avoiding a nuclear war, will measure their common interest, end their Cold War, and maintain together a stable world order, and condominium will succeed duopoly.

It is not an unworthy vision and, insofar as it now exists, represents an impressive diplomatic achievement, a sane and plausible resolution of the angry clash of volatile forces which characterized the world of the late 1940s.

But for all its benefits, the Cold War duopoly is unstable. It depends on a permanent tour de force by the superpowers, an effort which they will find difficult to sustain. Each has, in fact, been facing increasing resistance within its camp and has increasingly felt the strain within its own country.

In Eastern Europe, for example, the Russians face grave economic difficulties and strong recurring pressures for changes, including more intimate relations with the West—pressures whose moderation, if not supression, apparently requires periodic Russian military intervention. In Asia, the Russians fight alarming border skirmishes with a communist China. If America is more restrained, its camp is by no means tranquil. The Atlantic world is periodically shaken by economic, monetary, and political tensions.

Whatever the fate of the Russian and American military blocs in Europe, the superpowers are even less likely to maintain effective spheres of control over the jumble of new states in the Third World. Since the collapse of the old colonial system, this world has not been reforming into blocs under foreign tutelage, but fragmenting into independent particles.

It is hardly surprising, of course, that numerous particularist forces in the world, given the opportunity, should press for the dispersion of international power out of the postwar blocs. There seems also, however, a relative weakening of the superpowers themselves, and hence in their ability to resist the usual centrifugal forces. Why should this be so? One major cause lies in the very sphere in which their pre-eminence might seem especially assured, the sphere of military power. America and Russia are world giants by any conventional calculation. But their postwar predominance would seem far less decisive and durable without their massive superiority in nuclear weapons. Yet such has been the evolution of events that this kind of apocalyptic nuclear power, in which they are clearly so superior, is not easily translated into corresponding political, economic, or even military preponderance. Since World War II, there has grown up a kind of taboo against nuclear weapons, a taboo reinforced by numerous solid calculations of interest.[2] Because both America and Russia can absorb a heavy strike and still retaliate, neither can use its weapons against the other without inviting national suicide. Both, fearing an uncontrollable escalation, are shy of provoking any confrontation involving each other, and thus are strongly inhibited from threatening states in the other's camp. The inhibition extends, moreover, to nonaligned areas as well. Insofar as America and Russia imagine the world as a duopoly, they are inclined to see their competition in universal terms. Hence, one superpower's forceful incursion into a country often risks provoking the other to support the opposing side, or to bring pressure to bear somewhere else. Rather than risk such major confrontations, the superpowers are often surprisingly forebearing when minor powers commit outrages against their interest and dignity.

Even without the threat of confrontation, other inhibitions work against any full use of military power. To threaten lesser powers with nuclear weapons would seem barbaric and irresponsible; it would alienate public opinion and prompt other countries to seek nuclear weapons of their own. Because nuclear proliferation threatens duopoly and therefore the common interest of both superpowers, they have come together on the Nonproliferation Treaty and, again, as some people hope or fear, might ultimately move together toward a condominium. But both Russia and America have so far been too timid —partly, no doubt, because of their competitive fear of each other—actually to stop third countries from developing nuclear weapons.[3] Thus the superpowers appear unable to use their nuclear superiority, even to preserve it.

With their special source of superior power practically neutralized, the superpowers have had to operate in a prenuclear phantom world of traditional military, diplomatic, and economic resources, a world in which other actors also have the means to play considerable roles. Thus a middle power like France has been able to challenge American leadership in Western Europe, with some success, as well as build a small nuclear force of its own.

But France notwithstanding, military duopoly probably seems more real in Europe than anywhere else. It is in the Third World that the peculiar military impotence of the superpowers has become most strikingly apparent. Although the United States has managed successful military interventions elsewhere, the war in Vietnam has made clear the stupendously disproportionate margin of power needed to dominate a small and backward country when a sizable portion of its population is determined to resist. Thus, former colonial areas, in spite of their domestic instability and poverty, and their dependence on competitive blandishments, nevertheless achieve a great degree of liberty from external control, so much liberty in fact that many observers fear widespread international anarchy, especially if America's intervention in Southeast Asia is defeated decisively.

All these factors mean that the superpowers cannot effectively exercise their superior military resources. As a result, their world preponderance keeps eroding and its cost to them keeps rising. And as the costs rise, so do their domestic strains—strains which are becoming increasingly visible. Whatever the state of Soviet opinion, by the late 1960s a sizable portion of the American political elite, as well as the general public, appears to have decided that the country's international role was demanding a dangerously excessive proportion of its resources.

. It is fashionable to call this American domestic resistance neoisolationism. The term is misleading, if not disingenuous. The public figures associated with the movement—people like Fulbright, Kennedy, and Galbraith —are hardly prewar provincials. The broad movement that such men reflect is more properly called neohumanism than neoisolationism. It is prompted not by an American revulsion against foreigners, but by an American reaction against America. The United States, it is felt, is sacrificing the quality of its domestic life for the sake of external power. The urgent needs of the national society are being perilously neglected because the government is drunk with its world responsibilities. As a result of its steady domestic deterioration, America is becoming a country fit neither to live in nor to lead others. In the classic platonic syndrome, America is channeling its domestic violence and unhappiness into arrogance and aggression abroad. Unless drastic measures are taken to restore a sane proportion to national priorities, unless the militarization of the country is controlled, America will become a nightmare at home and a menace abroad.

Such sentiments a few years ago would have seemed extravagantly eccentric. Today they are commonplace. Evidence of the country's militarization is not difficult to find. Even the most sanguine booster of American ways can be disconcerted by the seemingly uncontrollable growth of the military budget in the past decade, up to a stunning $80 billion in 1968—10 percent of the country's GNP. At the same time, officials confidently predict that even ending the war in Vietnam will bring no overall reduction in military spending, that existing programs will by 1972 or 1973 absorb any conceivable savings.[4] New antiballistic missile systems and MIRVs (multiple independently targetable reentry vehicles) could easily raise costs in the 1970s well beyond their present totals.

Not only does this expenditure seem enormous, but it seems far beyond the reasonable requirements of national security in an era of at least partial détente. Since World War II, Americans have had a picture in their minds of the hordes from the East whose superior numbers were held at bay only by superior technology and, above all, by the nuclear deterrent. In fact, however, if there are any hordes, they appear to flow from the West rather than the East. In 1969, America's armed forces at 3,454,000 were actually larger than Russia's at 3,300,000 or China's at 2,500,000. The countries in NATO, other than the United States, had over 3 million men under arms as opposed to under 1.1 million for Russia's Warsaw Pact allies.[5] A 1968 Defense Department memorandum reckoned that the United States could "buy" all the forces of the Warsaw Pact, including Russia's, pay them at American scales, and build their equipment in American factories for $50 billion a year.[6] At that price, $30 billion would still remain in the American military budget, plus the additional $20 billion spent by America's European allies, to provide that marginal sufficiency which our customary definition of security requires.*

* Amid a flurry of statements announcing troop reductions and cuts in the military budget, the voice of the administration seemed to be speaking clearly. Henceforth, our military policy was to be based on "sufficiency" rather than "superiority," or, in practical terms, a capability to wage 1½ rather than 2½ wars simultaneously. *New York Times,* October 19, 1969; *Fortune,* December 1969. Secretary Laird soon rescued the doctrine from clarity: "The $80 billion was a realistic estimate as to what the Secretary of Defense and President felt could be spent in the defense area, but it was not enough to provide this country or put this country in a posture to handle two major wars and one minor war. If we price out where we are in our budget today, we are realistically in a position—*if we*

It is not surprising if some people, alarmed at clamorous domestic problems, want a drastic re-evaluation of America's priorities. Huge military expenditures inevitably influence the whole of national life. The defense industry represents a formidable proportion of industrial production and engages much of the country's most advanced technology and management.[7] Much of America's scientific manpower is preempted by military research. And there are also thousands of social scientists, in and out of universities, engaged directly or indirectly by the government in projects geared to buttressing America's military and diplomatic power. At a time when higher education in America seems to be on the verge of disintegration, the question naturally arises as to whether there are not more appropriate objects for the attention of the scholarly community.

Other costs are more difficult to count, but scarcely less significant. What is the effect of militarization on the general cultural mood of the nation? What is the relation between violence abroad and violence at home? More subtly, can a Hobbesian view of the international community, with order maintained chiefly by force, be

---

discount the present Vietnam situation—where we could support one major war and one minor conflict" (italics added). U.S., Congress, Senate Committee on Appropriations, *Hearings, Department of Defense Appropriations* (Washington, D.C., December 8, 1969), p. 60.

Rising to the challenge of the new rhetoric, Laird said: "I still like to believe that we should maintain a superior force in order to preserve an adequate or sufficient deterrent. I have not abandoned the use of that term, and I believe it is comprehended in my definition of the term 'sufficiency' or 'adequacy.' "

To which General Wheeler, chairman of the Joint Chiefs of Staff, added: "I, too, am one of the 'superiority' school of thinkers . . . and I think superiority should be understood in the context in which I use the word adequate. . . . I think our forces are 'adequate.' In other words, sufficiently superior in strength so that we can do these things." *Ibid.*, p. 88.

reconciled with a democratic vision of a domestic society based on consent? Can bureaucrats and politicians who think one way abroad think another way at home?

Such questions, and the anguish they entail, are nothing new in the world's history. Great powers have always felt the tensions between the needs of their imperium abroad and their nation at home. Many historians have reached the melancholy conclusion that external power is invariably bought at the expense of internal freedom. As Rome learned, empire and republic cannot co-exist. All these observations suggest an essential tension between America's foreign and domestic goals, between world responsibilities and domestic cultivation, between imperialism and democracy.

Such views are, of course, by no means universally accepted. There can be, it is frequently asserted, no security at home if there is no peace abroad.* And in the view of former President Johnson and many others, America has the resources for both world responsibility and domestic excellence. The majority of Americans, moreover, would doubtless deny that the United States has an empire.

Should America be called imperialist? There are obvious differences from one age to another in the mechanics and style of great-power "presence," economic and political "penetration," military "protection" or intervention, and direct and indirect rule. The American

---

* This principle is embedded in the rhetoric of the Truman Doctrine: "...totalitarian regimes imposed on free peoples, by direct or indirect aggression, undermine the foundations of international peace and hence the security of the United States." Similarly, President Johnson said, in his first major address after starting the bombing against North Vietnam: "We fight because we must fight if we are to live in a world where every country can shape its own destiny. And only in such a world will our freedom finally be secure." *Department of State Bulletin*, April 26, 1965, p. 606.

imperium, if that is what it should be called, certainly differs in its organization from the British empire in the early twentieth century, although it should not be overlooked just how much of that empire was made up of a self-governing Commonwealth linked primarily by economic, diplomatic, and cultural ties, and how much of what remained was left to the administration of cooperative native rulers. Indeed, as Hannah Arendt notes in her *Origins of Totalitarianism,* modern imperialism characteristically is contented to exercise selective control over certain key resources and policies while leaving the great bulk of the population, whenever possible, under native governments.[8] Modern imperialism seeks to gain control of key resources, markets, and strategic territories as cheaply as possible, that is, without having to assume the responsibility for government. Modern imperialism, as Miss Arendt would have it, thus tends to be more truly exploitative—precisely because it prefers to be indirect and irresponsible.

If imperialism is seen in this way, then the vast American apparatus of military protectorates, bases, and alliances, along with the great military power, the military and economic subsidies to foreign governments, the omnipresent diplomatic and intelligence network, the huge direct investments, and the preponderant position in the monetary system would seem to constitute a tolerable approximation of a modern empire.

Among scholars, the point is less and less disputed, not only among analysts who attack America's world role, but even among those who defend it. As America has come to assume the primary responsibility for world order, there is much more appreciation than formerly for the imperial role once played by the European states —much more tendency to see that role as responsibility rather than exploitation. Indeed, it has become commonplace to say that the United States has now inherited Britain's world role. Britain's domestic experience would seem to suggest no cause for despair over the fate in store for American democracy, for while the British empire presided over much of the world, Britain at home evolved into the most stable democracy in Europe.[9]

The parallel between Britain in the nineteenth century and America in the twentieth is not very exact, however much it may flatter both to affect a sort of modern day Donation of Constantine. It is instructive to consider the differences.

To begin with, it might be argued that the empire could not and did not survive Britain's becoming a genuine democracy at home. In any event, what makes the British experience so peculiar is the remarkable degree to which the whole imperial structure was insulated from the nation's domestic institutions. The seat of the empire was not at Westminster, but at Delhi. As the empire raised its own funds and soldiers from its own resources, Parliament had only the most sporadic control or surveillance. Thus the empire could remain an aristocracy while the kingdom became a democracy. Indeed, social adjustment in England was probably greatly assisted by the empire abroad. An aristocracy that was gradually losing its hold over domestic power found compensation in running an imperial bureaucracy overseas. The empire, like the Old West, provided a convenient outlet for the dissatisfied and the unwanted, and for aggressive enterprise of all sorts. Other countries less favorably endowed, the Germans for example, had to absorb men like Cecil Rhodes at home.

While imperialism might conceivably help draw off the racial tensions and general restlessness of American domestic society, it has had the opposite effect in the case of Vietnam. For one thing, the American involvements abroad are much more obviously competitive with domestic programs. The American empire is not self-supporting, but extremely expensive. It constantly competes for the funds needed for domestic improvements. This is not only because Americans are more profligate in their administration than the imperial British, but because the American empire is a vastly more pretentious burden.

The British empire, great as was its extent, based itself not so much on the inherent power of Britain, but on the peculiar weaknesses of others. There were two general conditions which made the empire possible for Britain, and which, as it happens, no longer exist for us. The first was a continental balance of power that engaged the resources of Britain's equals in a continuing general contest which none could win. Insular Britain could play the arbiter, ensuring that the continent's greater resources could never be united against her. The United States, on the other hand, has not yet found a way either in Europe or Asia to establish a local balance of power that contains her principal rivals. Far from being the outside arbiter, America is herself trapped in the game—and in two continents at once.

Secondly, Britain's empire was greatly favored by technological weakness and political apathy among not only the primitive societies of Africa but the normally advanced civilizations of Asia as well. Thus, the startling phenomenon of a middle-sized European state which came to govern half the world. The surprising thing is not that the empire ended, but that it lasted as long as it did. It was certainly not a fact of nature, and its demise did not leave an imperial vacuum waiting to be filled.

Today, in the Third World, political passivity has vanished and military technology no longer makes it easy to intervene. The conditions that helped Britain maintain an empire and build a democracy no longer exist. The *Pax Americana* places a much greater strain on domestic resources, in spite of their much greater abundance. The parallel, in short, is not between America and Britain but between America and Rome.

The British empire is said to have been acquired in a fit of absentmindedness. Americans, if not exactly absentminded, have scarcely been thought of as self-conscious Romans. Even enthusiastic advocates of an American imperium usually find it necessary, when they speak in public, to couch imperial ideas in the rhetoric of anticommunism, federalism, or even nationalism.[10] Indeed, this inhibition against an adequate imperial theory may be, as Vietnam suggests, the ultimate undoing of the American empire. A people accustomed to an extraordinary self-righteousness in their foreign policy will be increasingly difficult to rally without some acceptable popular theory that justifies the economic and moral burdens of American interventionism.

One source of inhibition against imperial theory lies in the rationale used initially to justify America's postwar involvements. The original apology drew not on the rhetoric of imperialism, but of nationalism—albeit a nationalism tempered by federalist cooperation. The Marshall Plan, for example, was made acceptable to the public and the Congress as a temporary catalyst for European self-help. America was not seeking to establish permanent dependencies, but to help others regain their strength. American money would be the seed capital to finance economic reconstruction. American power would be used to shield the rebuilding from the communist scavengers. American-sponsored multinational institutions would promote the habits needed to reconcile national independence with regional stability. As nations rebuilt and regions organized, there was to be a gradual devolution of American leadership and responsibility. Americans would go home, grateful applause ringing in their ears.

It has proved more difficult to give up power voluntarily than it was to acquire it unselfishly. Institutions like NATO have found it extremely difficult to transform themselves from channels of American leadership to instruments of European cooperation. The ideal of interdependence has given rise to the institution of dependence. Nation-building has, by way of alliance-building, become empire-building.

It would be dangerous for everyone, of course, if America's devolution turned into abrupt abdication. Yet as domestic and foreign anti-imperial pressures have increased almost irresistibly, the inability to devolve power rationally has led inexorably toward American collapse rather than devolution.

Why has it proved so difficult for America to complete its original world strategy? Why has America been unable to devolve gracefully from its assumption of primary responsibility and initiative in places where such vigorous interference might seem no longer essential? Most of the reasons are obvious enough. On the American side there has grown up an immense military and civil bureaucracy devoted to administering foreign commitments. The habits and routines of command are not easily given up without a very strong political will to override the inevitable inertia. Numerous other interests stand in the way. Arms manufacturers fear the loss of guaranteed markets. Professors of international relations fear the devaluation of old theories.

Nor are foreigners necessarily eager for American devolution. Many with long memories distrust their own national leadership and treasure their links with strong, democratic, and relatively stable America. Small countries prefer the gentle hegemony of a remote America to the more abrasive leadership of more immediate neighbors. Possessing classes want an anticommunist military presence to awe their own domestic radicals. For a great many individuals and countries, the American connections have been very profitable.

Hence there is no lack of ingenious arguments showing why America cannot disengage, or gloomy prophecies predicting what will happen if it does. It is not difficult, under the circumstances, to find or foster dissension among our clients, and to use it as evidence of disunity so hopeless that we cannot imagine anything but chaos without our active leadership.

All these factors are classic elements in the growth and persistence of empire. In the present world, there are some special factors as well. In spite of relaxations, Russia remains a respectably convincing common enemy —armed with a large army, a disagreeable political system, a revolutionary ideology with millions of foreign adherents, a vast apparatus for subversion, and an imperial system of her own.

The logic of nuclear defense introduces another special obstacle to cutting American commitments. As Russia has acquired a second-strike capacity to hit the continental United States with nuclear weapons, nuclear guarantees by the United States have taken on greater and greater risks. It is extremely difficult for those responsible for military planning to contemplate giving up close control over these local military situations that might lead to a nuclear confrontation.

In addition to these special military considerations, there are our own special ideological predilections. We project our own "federalist" political formula on international organizations, often, it almost seems, with the

U.S. government unconsciously expecting to take the same role abroad as it does at home. Reluctant allies are seen as retrograde states' righters, obstructing the juggernaut of federal progress. Americans are much bemused by the rather vacant concept of a "world rule of law," without much consideration about its political, social, and cultural preconditions. In general, the American imagination abroad shows, for a democratic people, a remarkable unconsciousness about the need for political consensus as the broad foundation for governments and laws. Good institutional superstructures are all that seem necessary.

. Added to this insensitivity about the difference between politics and machinery is the national weakness for rhetorical inflation. Particular arrangements constantly escalate into universal principles. Hence the Truman Doctrine to defend Greece and Turkey became a commitment to defend free peoples everywhere. There is the recurring cycle of apocalyptic expectations and exaggerated disappointments that typify America's relations with international organizations like the United Nations or the Alliance for Progress. When the expectations are thwarted in one institution, they migrate to another. Hence the remarkable ideological baggage carried around by NATO. America suffers from an oversupply of short-term moral capital, an excessive ideological liquidity which constantly distorts the marketplace of ideas. It leads, moreover, to that constant tendency to overcommitment which characterizes so many of our involvements.

In recent years, however, there has been no shortage of sophisticated justifications for America's foreign role. These arguments have evolved from the containment of communism to the general preservation of "world order" and a balance of power everywhere. Destiny, it is said, has given the United States a catalytic role in the creation of a new world order—to be based not on naïve utopian hopes, but on the reality of American power, enforcing, with the occasional aid of a posse of allies, the gradually evolving body of rules for international conduct that began with the Truman Doctrine. If these ideas have had a limited popular appeal, they have had a great influence in official and academic circles.

With these developments in theory, ideology has at last caught up with practice. Both are without limit. The original notion of a temporary mission as a special policeman has evolved into a permanent job of world sheriff.

The notion that power corrupts—or ennobles—is scarcely new. It is not surprising that American soldiers, bureaucrats, and politicians find it difficult to disengage from the positions of power that were theirs for the taking twenty years ago. Perhaps we are therefore doomed to become an empire. Perhaps we should renounce our Arcadian domestic aspirations and take up the imperial mantle in a fashion to do us credit before the appraising eye of history.[11] No doubt, worse things could happen to us and to the world. In any event, whatever our attempted policies, we shall have to manage, well or ill, an inevitably extensive international position.

The experience of Vietnam suggests, however, an urgent need for a reapportionment between the moral and physical demands of domestic health, on the one hand, and international duty, on the other. For the gravest invitation to genuine neoisolationism in America —to a catastrophic abandonment of foreign commitments—lies in those undisciplined imperialist pretensions that constitute a real threat both to democratic society in America and to peace in the world. It is our inability to measure our international role against our own resources, and those of others, that will drive America to the tragic choice between isolationism abroad or repression at home. All this is easy enough to say in the abstract. But how can our external commitments be cut back?

Faced with pressures for retrenchment, there is an understandable tendency to try to maintain the same positions abroad, only more cheaply. But we should have learned by now that partial disengagements from leadership are difficult to manage. Either we turn over the primary initiative for their own defense to others, or they continue as indolent and entangling dependencies. Our original strategy of reconstruction followed by withdrawal was a more promising course. If we could apply it in some place of significance, we should not only reduce the mounting strain on our resources, but mark a new direction in the conduct of our foreign policy—a renunciation not of commitments and duties, but of pretensions to empire. As a self-conscious, symbolic act, such a step would not only reduce American discontent with remaining burdens, but also mitigate and condition our active hegemony in those parts of the world where it might still seem essential.

Is there any part of the world ripe for devolution? At the present time, Asia, no doubt, seems the most promising candidate. The military intervention in Vietnam has been a depressing failure. It at least proves that if military power is to play any useful role in our diplomacy, we need military doctrines, formulations, and leadership appropriate to the political policy which the military intervention is meant to be serving. But because the intervention has been handled badly—or even because it was unnecessary to begin with—does not necessarily prove that we can withdraw from our Asian commitments. In those parts of the world that have suffered from all the shocks of war, decolonization, westernization, and communism, it is unrealistic to assume that the United States will not have to continue an energetic, if more selective, role. Indeed, few serious students of foreign affairs, whatever their views on Vietnam, deny the continuing necessity for an active American role among the crowd of heterogeneous new states that have replaced the old European empires. The unstructured and unsettled situation in the Third World generally suggests that the prospects for more than tactical and provisional disengagement will remain uncertain for some time. In short, Asia is not the place for a dramatic renunciation of American leadership, even if it is now time to begin seriously fostering a local balance that will allow devolution in the future.

Europe is a different story. In many respects, Western Europe today offers a splendid prospect for a major reduction in American responsibilities. It was in Western Europe that the original strategy of buying time and withdrawing was formulated. By now Western European resources are collectively as great, if not greater, than those of the Soviet Union. The principal countries have stable democratic regimes and well-equipped armies. The Common Market suggests great skill in managing intimate cooperation among governments. While most Europeans want an Atlantic Alliance, many are restive at America's continuing hegemony in NATO, and some fear that it prevents the long-delayed general European political settlement.

For Americans, devolution in Europe would offer many benefits. Our European commitments are extremely costly. Moreover, it is in the institutions of the alliance with Western Europe that American federalist tendencies have produced their most elaborate fantasies —where the needs of interdependence and the aspirations of empire have become most insidiously mixed. A clear, self-conscious renunciation of American imperial pretensions in Europe would therefore greatly clarify America's vision of itself in the world. If we cannot at least turn away from pretensions to hegemony in Europe, where we are not needed, the prospect for a rational devolution of our swollen international responsibilities is unlikely anywhere. History will have caught us in empire and the American dream will have given way to the American century.

From both sides of the Atlantic the opposition to such a renunciation will be clamorous, and certainly not lacking in either sincerity or intelligence. NATO and all the other institutions of the Atlantic connection are the most obvious and impressive monuments to American success in this postwar era. Clearly, it will be said, they are not to be thrown away in some burst of fitful experimentation. Nothing, it seems, paralyzes the imagination so much as an old and decaying success.

II. NATO: ILLUSIONS AND REALITIES

NATO is more than twenty years old. Along with the Berlin Wall, it is probably the world's principal monument to the Cold War. Though it has been in "disarray" almost since it was built, it is still standing, like those tenacious temporary buildings on the Mall in Washington, and enthusiasts expect it still to be standing twenty years hence. Why has it endured? Is it perhaps the harbinger of a new Atlantic community, or is it merely an institutional remnant of America's postwar hegemony? In the beginning, was it meant to be a temporary protectorate, or the first step toward a federated "Atlantica"?

While a study of its origins in the Cold War tells a good deal about NATO's present character, it does not necessarily clarify the intent of the founders. Ambiguity has been NATO's heritage from the very beginning.[1] People have found in it whatever they were looking for. For the enlightened isolationist, it meant a shield, at first only a verbal promise of support, behind which the ravaged Europeans could rebuild their strength so that Americans could go home. For Secretary of State Acheson, on the other hand, NATO was the product of at least 350 years of history, perhaps more. It joined "the two halves of what is in reality one community"—a community inspired by "common institutions and moral and ethical beliefs" and "the effect of living on the sea."[2]

Another prominent witness to NATO's birth, George Kennan, says he found the whole enterprise a misguided perversion of "containment."[3] NATO violated, Kennan believed, the sound principle of the Marshall Plan: "that they set up their own organization and that we appear as the great and good friends, but not participating members of what they had set up." Furthermore, Kennan found NATO militarily unnecessary and wasteful of resources needed for political and economic recovery. As for the official rhetoric behind it, it was "typical of that mixture of arid legalism and semantic pretentiousness that so often passes, in the halls of our domestic political life, for statesmanship."[4]

The treaty's text is itself a contribution to NATO's heritage of ambiguity. It is a surprisingly ambivalent document considering how much has been built upon it.* Testimony in the Senate before ratification minimized the possibility of any American troop commitment, stressing instead our political and cultural ties with Europe. Secretary of State Dean Acheson, when asked if we were expected to send substantial troops abroad permanently, responded with a "clear and absolute 'no.' "[5] The treaty, moreover, was careful to limit the commitment, such as it is, to an attack within the treaty area.

To be sure, the treaty of 1949 is a good deal less than the organization built upon its foundation in 1951. Although the treaty does provide for a Council and permits it "subsidiary bodies," the present luxuriant institutional growth—the Supreme Allied Commanders and their integrated staffs—were all later additions.[6] It was the Korean invasion, in June of 1950, that precipitated the evolution of NATO from a transatlantic mutual assistance treaty into an integrated military alliance, run

---

* While "an armed attack against one or all of them in Europe or North America shall be considered an attack against them all," each party is pledged only to take "such action as it deems necessary, including the use of armed force, to restore and maintain the security of the North Atlantic area."

by the United States. Thus NATO was born in two distinct stages, which helps explain further some of its ambiguity of character and purpose.

The organizational pattern created in 1950 is essentially the pattern that exists in 1970. The treaty's organization provides parallel military and political structures. The military structure is built around the three supreme commands—Europe, Atlantic, and the Channel. The political structure is grouped around the Council of fifteen permanent representatives and its various strategic and logistical committees.

The considerable difference between NATO's rhetoric and practice further contributes to the prevailing ambiguity. According to its more ardent propagandists, NATO's structure, ideally, is informed by two fundamental postulates: First, it is said that the defense of the United States and Western Europe is indivisible—that so vital is Western Europe to us that we are prepared to defend it as we would ourselves, in other words, all the way to a full-scale nuclear war bringing catastrophic destruction to our own homeland.[7] Presumably we expect our European partners to share an equal interest in the defense of the United States. Second, it is assumed that the successful management of our common defense requires the integrated political and military structure of NATO.

Ideally these two postulates determine the way NATO works. The common soil of the Atlantic community is protected by the umbrella of integrated common defense. The common strategy is hammered out in the NATO Council, the Alliance's political master. SACEUR and the other commanders are the Council's military stewards, directing the pooled citizen-armies. The United States, of course, does retain national control over the nuclear umbrella, but American plans and strategies for Europe's defense are the product of intensive consultation among partners. The guiding principle of the whole enterprise is interdependence, organized effectively through institutions that tie the partners to common decisions and integrate their forces.*

In practice, however, NATO's interdependence is rather selective in its application. Indeed, integration is illusory in many respects, which only serves to compound the ambiguous and unreal atmosphere of the institution. To begin with, the political institutions have little authority over the military. If, in theory, the Council is the political master and SACEUR the military steward, in practice, even strong partisans of NATO see little integration between the political machinery and the military commands. Hence the Council has never functioned as the Alliance's principal center for policy making, or even consultation. The Council's role has always been peripheral to the military machinery built up around the Supreme Allied Commander. This lack of integration between the political authority and the military command has led one famous observer, General Beaufre, to call NATO "a body without a head."[8] But there is a head—not in Europe, but in Washington.

The Supreme Allied Commander has never been the first servant of the Council, but the viceroy of the American president. As a viceroy, to be sure, he may sometimes come to champion the provincial views in his own domain as opposed to the global perspectives pre-

---

* "The practice of political consultation which has developed over the years is now established as an indispensable element in the functioning of the Alliance. Its significance, not least for the smaller NATO countries, can hardly be overestimated. It provides the opportunity for all member countries to take full part in the shaping of the major policies of the Western world—regardless of size or power." NATO Information Service, *NATO, Facts and Figures* (Brussels, 1969), p. 96.

vailing at the imperial center.[9] Nevertheless, he is a man from the center, and it is from Washington that his ultimate authority comes, for Washington controls the nuclear weapons everyone believes constitute the real defense of Europe. The line of nuclear authority passes directly from Washington to the American military commander in Europe, who, almost necessarily, is also SACEUR.

The strategic defense of America and Europe may be indivisible, and NATO may be a collective umbrella, but only the American president can decide when to put it up. In short, the decisive weapons for NATO's defense are not subject to integration, but are under direct American control.

To come down to it, NATO's command arrangements reflect the fundamental assumption that the primary responsibility and ultimate direction for European defense should be held by the Americans. NATO is the rather elaborate apparatus by which we have chosen to organize the American protectorate over Europe. In practice, the arrangements reflect dependence and not interdependence, hegemony and not integration.

There is, to be sure, a good deal of apparent integration in the whole elaborate military staff apparatus. NATO's Supreme Headquarters in Europe (SHAPE) is a babble of uniforms and accents greatly pleasing to the multinational taste. But the degree of genuine integration in the military command is easily exaggerated.* It is hard to escape the observation that NATO's integrated command is largely an Anglo-Saxon affair.[10] Of

---

* General André Beaufre, French representative to the Military Standing Group in 1960, describes it as "an encysted organism . . . a system of wheels without power revolving almost endlessly around questions of routine." Beaufre, *NATO and Europe* (New York, 1966), p. 33.

the three main commands in NATO, two, SACEUR and SACLANT—have always been held by Americans, while the third—the Channel Command—is a British preserve. Of the thirteen major subordinate commands, British or American officers have from the beginning held all but two.

In effect, integration in NATO theoretically means that France and Germany, with the largest European armies and air forces, are to be subject to American commands in defense of their own homelands—sharing a common integrated subordination with the Belgians, Dutch, Greeks, Italians, Turks, and Portuguese. Only the British would preserve primacy in their own home defense, extending it to Norway. Thus the integration of NATO commands is a rather selective expression of nationalist capitulation before interdependence. General de Gaulle's views aside, it would be surprising if the French military had developed less than warm enthusiasm for the benefits of command integration under NATO.

In short, NATO, which in theory suggests interdependence, integration, and a potential federation, in practice involves dependence, subordination, and potential empire. It would, that is, if NATO had any real authority over the military forces of the European partners. In fact, it does not, which is yet another confusing element in the situation.

NATO's organizational inequities are very likely tolerated as much as they are because the actual authority of its "integrated" commands is only hypothetical. National governments assign NATO whatever forces they please[11] and retain sovereign control even over these forces until persuaded to integrate for an emergency. In this respect NATO is not so much a body without a head as it is a kind of military central nervous system, lacking not only a head, but a body as well.[12] With the exception of Germany, the major European powers have assigned only a limited proportion of their armies to NATO. From the start, the British, as a world power, kept a major part of their forces outside. In the 1950s the French used the great bulk of their armies to fight two major colonial wars, neither of which involved the NATO command, although one was fought in the Mediterranean. Lesser powers have been similarly uninhibited by their NATO commitment. In 1964, Greece and Turkey prepared for war with each other almost entirely with troops assigned, on both sides, to the American commander of AFSOUTH in Naples.[13]

What, it might be asked, is all this for? It is fair to say that if the Russian army ever does advance into Europe, it will be the most elaborately anticipated and least expected invasion in Europe's history. NATO is sold as a kind of Noah's Ark, but no one in it expects any rain. Even Europeans who believe the worst about Russian intentions do not expect them to attack in the face of the American threat to use nuclear weapons—a threat backed up by a sizable contingent of American forces and 7,000 nuclear weapons in the path of the putative Russian invaders. Thus, to many Europeans, NATO's one-sided integration, mostly theoretical anyway, seems a small price to pay for the American nuclear deterrent.

In summary, there is a good deal less to NATO than meets the eye. With all its industrious committees and bloated staffs, NATO might seem an elaborate charade, designed to humor the American penchant for daydreaming with organizational charts.[14] While it is true that in NATO the Americans preach integration but practice hegemony, their control in fact extends over a series of bureaucratic staffs which in themselves have no real authority over national forces, and which exist solely to plan for an invasion that no one expects. Troops for NATO, moreover, cost the Americans some billion and a half dollars annually in foreign exchange[15] —all helping to bolster European payments balances. No wonder the rest of the Europeans were furious with de Gaulle for threatening the illusions, for telling the emperor he had no clothes.

What makes the existing NATO situation even more ironical and unreal is that the existing conventional military forces that might be available to NATO are probably stronger than those available to the Warsaw Pact. Yet while NATO's propagandists constantly vaunt an integration which is in fact illusory, they constantly deplore the weakness of Western Europe's actual forces.

Ever since the beginning, people have been worried by NATO's failure to reach the minimum force goals set by its own Council. Originally, planners spoke hopefully of 100 divisions. At the Lisbon Conference in 1952, the NATO Council solemnly called for 96. By 1954, the Council was ready to settle for 70. More significantly, there were to be 30 active divisions on the Central Front. But on that Front, NATO has, in fact, never gone beyond 25. In early years, part of the blame lay with the reigning doctrine of massive retaliation.[16] But in 1969, even after several years of a flexible response strategy emphasizing conventional forces, NATO in Central Europe still had only 24 divisions.

By the late 1960s, experts began to decide that NATO's apparent failure had no great military significance. In early 1968, the Secretary of Defense published an assessment declaring NATO's conventional forces capable of stopping anything short of a full-scale non-nuclear attack.[17] NATO's land forces were thought roughly equal to their opponents, and their tactical air forces markedly superior. An authoritative Defense Department memorandum, released in October 1968, came to the same conclusions and decided that any relative weaknesses sprang not from inadequate resources, but from "readiness deficiencies NATO has not thought worth fixing."[18]

After years of emphasizing the Russian horde, held back only by the threat of massive nuclear retaliation, this suddenly cheerful view excited considerable popular surprise, if not incredulity.[19] But no one should be astonished if the NATO countries match the Warsaw Pact countries in conventional military strength. As I have noted, in 1969 the Soviet Union had slightly smaller military forces than the United States: 3,300,000 as opposed to 3,454,000.[20] True, the United States has its worldwide commitments, including over half a million men in Vietnam, but the Russians share a border of 4,500 miles with 800 million angry Chinese.*

And if America and Russia are roughly equal, their respective European allies most certainly are not. America's NATO's allies have over 3 million men under arms, compared to less than 1.1 million for Russia's Warsaw Pact allies. Among Western Europeans, the forces of the major powers—Britain, France, and the Federal Republic of Germany—alone total nearly 1.4 million men. On the Central Front, the armed forces of Russia's Warsaw Pact allies total 230,000 Czechs, 137,000 East Germans, and 275,000 Poles—together only 642,000, and comparable to the Western Europeans neither in technical competence nor in political reliability. In the southeast, the support for the Soviets

---

* On the Chinese border, Russians are believed to have about 270,000 troops in 30 divisions, as against a rapid potential Chinese deployment of over one million men. Institute for Strategic Studies, *Strategic Survey* (London, 1970), pp. 71–72.

is even weaker. Forces of NATO countries adjacent to the Balkans include 420,000 Italians, 159,000 Greeks, and 483,000 Turks, against which the Russians might hope to employ combined Hungarian, Bulgarian, and Rumanian forces of 444,000.[21]

Looked at from the Russian side, the conventional military balance can hardly appear favorable at all, and certainly not favorable enough to try for a quick military victory. To overcome this western margin, the Russians would have to move a gigantic force from their interior armies. Movements on so grand a scale would necessarily be apparent several weeks in advance, as they were for the relatively minor displacement required for the Czech invasion.* In short, if NATO's conventional defense is somehow inadequate, the problem arises not from any lack of military resources, but from the political difficulties among the allies. Ironically it is America's hegemonic integration, so illusory anyway, which has split the Alliance and dispersed Western Europe's real military strength.

The only serious attack NATO has ever faced was not military but political, and came not from Russia but from France.

In 1966, the French, while professing to remain in the Alliance, withdrew from its military organization.

---

* There was no secret about Warsaw Pact and Russian mobilization well before the Czech intervention itself. In mid-June, Russians conducted "joint exercises" on Czech soil, leaving behind large numbers of troops as well as sophisticated radio and communications equipment. In mid-July, Russia announced Pact exercises which were noted in the western press as being unusually large, involving Russian rear-line troops and reservists as well as regular Pact forces. The West responded by moving NATO exercises scheduled for September from the Czech border to southwest Germany. See, for example, *The Economist*, May 11, 1968, p. 41; July 13, 1968, p. 30; and July 27, 1968, pp. 18–20.

They took out not only their assigned forces, but ordered SHAPE and AFCENT headquarters to move off French soil, evacuate all their bases there, and abandon the use of the supply infrastructure built up over the years.[22] While it was said that the use of French land, airspace, and general facilities might possibly be secured by negotiation in time of a crisis, NATO could not count on their automatic use.[23]

If anyone takes these military matters seriously, it must be seen that a neutral or hostile France would make NATO's military position unenviable.[24] Despite the bold face of the experts, without France NATO has no plausible conventional deterrent, and no primarily European defense of Europe is really imaginable.

Over three years have gone by since the French withdrawal. Nothing very dramatic has happened. The Russians have not invaded. NATO is officially said to be stronger than ever. Its multitudinous committees reach agreement more often. Apathy is doubtless expeditious. Moreover, relations between France and America have improved considerably, and de Gaulle's departure has perhaps created a more hopeful mood on both sides. But beneath its bustling front the Alliance is bleeding from a grievous wound.

America is the loser. If our hegemonic authority is no longer openly challenged, the relative burden for European defense has been shifted even more to our shoulders. Given Europe's own impressive military resources, America's present commanding role is scarcely necessary to counterbalance the Russians, if the Europeans would take their own defense seriously. If the goal of our foreign policy is to reduce burdens where we can, we have suffered a major defeat. Whether the defeat is our fault is another matter. Whether a reformed NATO could hold Gaullist France, or whether some European defense coalition is now possible—these are the complex questions taken up in the pages that follow.

One point needs to be made here: insofar as the Alliance's split results from our attachment to NATO's deceptive formula of integration, we have paid a heavy price for our intellectual enslavement to a heritage of ambiguity and illusion.

Why then are we so firmly attached to these formulas? Why has NATO developed in so apparently self-defeating a fashion? Why have we so much difficulty imagining it organized in any other way? The answer lies rather deep. A nation's policies are determined not only by the exigencies and possibilities of the outside world, but by the peculiar qualities of its own political imagination—by the way its leaders and people perceive the world beyond and present to themselves its challenges, dangers, and opportunities. For the past twenty-five years, the American imagination has fixed itself in a certain pattern, a pattern that has now become so institutionalized in countless doctrines, arrangements, and reputations that it pervades even the minds of those who oppose it. As a first step toward liberation, it might be useful to go back briefly to the Cold War itself to see how we have come to see the world as we do.

III. THE COLD WAR AND THE BIRTH OF NATO

As they examine it in the calm light of historical retrospection, a great many contemporary historians find the Cold War strangely improbable. To an unusual degree, all sides seem to have been prisoners not so much of the exigencies of their national and personal positions, as of the illusions of their own limited imaginations. Many historians, for example, agree with Louis Halle that postwar western fears of Russia were greatly exaggerated: "By 1948, the general view in the West was that, in accordance with communist ideology, Stalin had the domination of the entire world as his goal. In fact, as we know, the forces under his leadership were going beyond where he wanted them to go."[1]

Even if both sides had understood each other perfectly, there was plenty of cause for conflict, if not for a Cold War. The descent of totalitarianism over proud and civilized nations in Eastern Europe was, and remains, ample cause to detest Stalin and his blood-stained tyranny. The difference between a totalitarian police state and a free society was clear enough, especially for Europeans near or beyond the edge of the western pale.[2] But, in return, revisionist historians point up the official ambitions and pressures for an American economic penetration eastward, which, if successful, would clearly have undermined Russian influence in Eastern Europe and might well have threatened the continuation of a communist society in Russia itself.[3]

In any event, it is difficult to deny that Russia's posture was menacing. But the proposition that Russia's brutal extension over peoples on her western border constituted the first step in a Soviet design to dominate all Europe, and then all the world, must inevitably arouse some skepticism. There are, after all, less exalted explanations. Russia had suffered a massive invasion from Germany twice in twenty-five years. The traditional uncooperativeness and frequent hostility of Russia's immediate neighbors, while entirely understandable from the neighbors' point of view, was not conducive to Russian security. Stalin's ambition for an Eastern European *glacis* of puppets cannot have seemed unreasonable to him. After all, as he remarked, he never complained that the new government in Belgium was unrepresentative. Indeed, if several unfriendly accounts are to be believed, Stalin had a healthy respect for the vital interests of his major wartime allies and not infrequently restrained the exuberance of other more revolutionary communist governments and parties.[4]

For all his domestic paranoia, Stalin is widely admitted to have played the international game rationally and with prudence. Even his fears, though inflated by crafty madness, were not entirely unreasonable. Some in the West did think of a separate peace with Germany. Perhaps more should have. Others apparently did speculate about using our nuclear monopoly to force fundamental changes in Russia's policies.[5] One might have wished them greater success. And if Stalin saw bad faith and devious designs where there was only confusion and naïveté, the fault was not entirely his. To quote from the judgments of the distinguished Harvard historian, Adam Ulam: "Having ... seemingly sealed a bargain, the Anglo-American statesmen would revert to wrangling and moral admonitions. The problem remained, over and above the question of Soviet objections and ruthless methods, one of communication; at times it must have been as difficult for Stalin to understand what his allies really wanted as it was for Churchill and Roosevelt to understand the alleged enigmas and puzzles of Soviet policy."[6]

Soviet-American relations deteriorated after Yalta because of Stalin's policy in Eastern Europe. Poland, above all, poisoned the atmosphere of the Grand Alliance—to the puzzlement and irritation of the Russians: "In Teheran, on their own initiative, the Western Powers had conceded all the essential points of the Polish issue. What was the subsequent wrangling about unless it meant the United States and Britain were concocting some scheme or going back on their word?"[7]

Stalin's irritations were understandable. He could hardly have anticipated American naïveté about what he would do when given a free hand. Western armies, after all, were not beyond suppressing local communists.[8] Certainly Churchill gave few signs of ignorance about communist methods. Yet at Teheran in 1943 it was Churchill who first proposed recognizing Russian sway in Warsaw.[9] The bargains were struck freely; good relations between Russia and the West depended on their being kept. Yet to Stalin, the West appeared to be regretting its promises.

Even if Stalin had been far more experienced with the West, and a good deal less paranoid, it is doubtful if he would ever have understood Roosevelt's various world visions. Even if he had, there was little chance for the open and friendly partnership between American democracy and Soviet totalitarianism which appears to have played so large a part in the President's dreams. Ironically it was America's naïve regard for Russia which led the two countries to a Cold War rather than to the guarded accommodation which ought to have been possible.

Defending Stalin's awesome domestic tyranny will always remain an uncongenial task for even the most fervent revisionist. Nevertheless, there was generally an inner logic, however terrible, in Stalin's domestic policies. Indeed, as our own depressing experience with "nation-building" in backward countries continues, more people may develop a sneaking admiration for Stalinist efficiency, or at least a greater tolerance for totalitarian methods under such unpromising circumstances. But there will always be an air of savage madness over Stalin's Russia that no rational thesis can entirely explain away.

The mad paranoic fear never mellowed. Instead, after World War II it grew worse.* From 1945 to 1953 Russia endured a period of pathological hostility and isolation unmatched even in the worst days of the interwar period. Under the circumstances, normal international intercourse was out of the question, let alone such intimacy as participation in the Marshall Plan. But Russia's menacing hostility, so inexplicable to an America eager for cooperation, had a rational basis, even if it was also congenial to Stalin's temperament. As a policy, however,

---

* Stalin's daughter Svetlana describes his last years thus: "Spiritually drained, with all human attachments forgotten, stalked by fear, which in the last few years grew into a genuine persecution mania, his nerves of steel at last gave way. Yet his mania was no sick fancy; he knew that he was hated, and he knew why. Finally, cut off by his power, his glory, his semi-paralyzed consciousness, from life and people, he sent them from his death bed what he could: a look full of terror and rage, and a threatening gesture of his hand." Svetlana Alliluyeva, *Only One Year* (New York, 1969), pp. 141–76. See also Adam Ulam, *Expansion and Coexistence* (New York, 1968), p. 402.

the menacing was not the expression of expansionist vigor, as the West feared, but of conservative fright.*

For all the prestige of its arms, Russia suffered a most terrible destruction in World War II. Up to 20 million people had been killed. The entire western half of the country was in ruins. The Russian people, whom Stalin, it is said, never expected would save his regime, nevertheless fought for it with a stubborn determination which aroused the wonder and admiration of the world. But Stalin held out no relaxation for his unexpectedly loyal subjects. The stupendous task of rebuilding would demand more hardship and more discipline, and it was possible only in a society kept isolated and terrified.[10] Otherwise Russia could never catch up with the Americans, for whom the war had been the occasion for fantastic growth rather than widespread destruction. Russia, like Western Europe, would lose her self-determination and be swept up into the new international system dominated by American capitalism.

Under the circumstances, Stalin scarcely had in mind the program of universal communist domination with which so many in the West frightened themselves. Least of all, considering America's nuclear superiority, did he seriously plan the military thrust into Western Europe which NATO so ponderously sought to counter. As Kennan argued at the time, the West was threatened by

---

* "From the beginning in the ninth century, and even today, the prime driving force in Russia has been fear. Fear, rather than ambition, is the principal reason for the organization and expansion of the Russian society. . . . From the days of Ivan the Great until our own time, a period of five centuries, the history of Moscow is one of steady, continuing expansion. Yet this expansion, in a way peculiar to Russia, is not an aggressive expansion. Right up to our own day it is a defensive expansion, an expansion prompted by the lack of natural defensive frontiers in a world of mortal dangers on all sides." Louis J. Halle, *The Cold War as History* (New York, 1967), pp. 12–17.

its own economic and political weakness, not by the Red Army.*

Indeed, Soviet forces demobilized rapidly. If Khrushchev is to be believed, and several noted western scholars accept his figures, by 1948 Russian armed forces had dropped from 11,365,000 to 2,874,000, a surprisingly low figure considering the army's essential role in the Eastern European satellites. There were no substantial increases until after Stalin's death in 1953.[11]

Behind the policies of open brutality in Eastern Europe, harsh polemics at the United Nations, subversion and menace worldwide, blockades in Berlin, and wars in Korea,[12] the Russian position, weak at home and so stretched abroad, was exceedingly vulnerable. Stalin was not the first to discover that offense is the best defense. As Ulam observes: "A Russia adhering to the Marshall Plan, 'behaving' in the United Nations, pursuing a more liberal policy in her Eastern European sphere of influence, would have been much less an object of fear, much more susceptible to pressure and outside challenges than the mysterious and threatening colossus seemingly ready to unleash countless hordes upon a defenseless Europe."[13]

Stalin's policy, however natural to him and to his regime, was a cruel defeat for the ideals that had sustained America through the war. Wartime propaganda and Russian heroism had papered over the horrors and made the Russians popular. Moreover, Roosevelt's plans for postwar world organization required Russian-American cooperation as the indispensable precondition.[14]

* For Kennan, the worrisome communist behavior in late 1947 and 1948 was a "predictable baring of the fangs" in response to such western initiatives as the Marshall Plan. George F. Kennan, *Memoirs* (Boston, 1967), p. 403. The European desire for a transatlantic military alliance was an unneeded and dangerous diversion from economic recovery to military rivalry, p. 408.

American federalist daydreams in this period, heightened by the great strains and abandoned emotions of wartime, reached a dangerous degree of unreality. For example, so little was the character of the Russian regime understood that the Treasury Department was apparently stupefied to learn that Stalin would not let Russia join the IMF![15] That many American expectations of the new universal world order were impossibly naïve did not make their ultimate disappointment any less bitter, or the subsequent reaction any less excessive.[16]

When the popular reaction against Russia finally came to this country, it touched off a dangerously violent surge of anticommunist witch-hunting. The Russians were seen to be following a master plan for world domination. A vast armed horde was thought poised to sweep over Western Europe, while French and Italian communists unlocked the gates.

Once jolted from illusions, America's reaction was massive. Many of Truman's policies were well-conceived. The Marshall Plan spurred economic rebuilding and made a generous gesture toward reuniting Europe. Doubtless a new firmness toward probings in Greece, Turkey, and Iran was salutary. But the new ideological baggage was dangerous. The American imagination immediately began to construct a new world of illusions. The prudent policy of containment gradually was translated into a new world order. The soaring rhetoric of the Truman Doctrine committed the United States all around the world to "support free people who are resisting attempted subjection by armed minorities or by outside pressures."[17] Armed with so sweeping a principle, the lawyers set to work to build, starting with NATO, the series of pacts and treaty organizations that were soon to girdle the globe. Thus they institutionalized the confrontation in Europe, such as it was, and spread it everywhere else. The federal spirit, disgusted with the wrangling United Nations, migrated to NATO.

Paranoid or not, the Russians might have been forgiven for deciding that so vast a western effort was aimed at their destruction. But the reality was far better than they deserved. Stalin's aggressive defense succeeded all too well. American paranoia began to match his own. America's formidable energies turned not against Russia, but to institutionalizing its own bloc. The United States became obsessed with building a new kind of Maginot Line, an institution whose chief effect was to imprison its defenders.

As the United States built a defensive Atlantic community, Russia recovered domestically, developed nuclear weapons of her own, and consolidated her hold over Eastern Europe. Thus, at the time of Russia's greatest internal weakness, nothing serious was done to probe her extended position in Eastern Europe. And later, when a new Russian regime, beset by domestic and foreign divisions, showed signs of wanting a European political settlement, the West was too preoccupied with its fortifications to take notice.[18] The arbitrary and accidental division down the middle of Germany became the iron boundary between two hostile and isolated worlds. The work of centuries was undone—Europe returned to a division that had not existed since the fall of Rome.

America and Russia, meanwhile, had become "a scorpion and a tarantula together in a bottle"—to use Halle's striking metaphor: "For the moment, at least, no understanding between them is possible. If either stopped fighting, he would immediately be killed. From the point of view of each, the basic situation is that the other is trying to kill him. . . . The situation is tragic. The proper attitude of the observer, therefore, is one of sympathy for both sides."[19]

But what are we to say when, over twenty years afterward, as sane and knowledgeable an analyst of American foreign policy as Seyom Brown can still summarize the pervasive premise among top levels of American policy makers as follows: "The Soviet Union is motivated [how strongly is a variable] ... eventually to fashion the world into a single political system based on the Soviet model. The premise that the Soviets are motivated only to secure their society against outside interference has never been bought at the highest levels of the United States government since the Second World War."[20]

To return to Halle's metaphor: perhaps it is time for more than sympathy. Perhaps it is time to break the bottle. Indeed, Mr. Halle has himself cast a sizable stone.

V. THE CONSOLIDATION AND DISINTEGRATION OF THE ATLANTIC BLOC

Once formed out of the Cold War, NATO proceeded according to its own logic, the logic inherent in an American nuclear protectorate for Western Europe. The 1950s, a period of regional concentration in the world's state system, provided a generally favorable climate for NATO's development and consolidation. It was a decade when both superpowers built elaborate systems of client states, while those neutrals who sought escape from duopoly often tried building blocs of their own. Strategically, it was a defensive age, even if the tactics were often aggressive. No one wanted a major war—not surprising after what the world had been through in the 1940s and what nuclear weapons promised for the future.

There were, of course, occasional Soviet-American "confrontations." The desire of both superpowers to extend into uncommitted areas or to take advantage of the chaos of decolonization resulted in a great deal of competitive probing, tension, unpleasantness, and now and then a more serious clash. Nevertheless, both sides drew back from head-on collisions. Even Korea appears to have been a misunderstanding rather than a deliberate challenge.[1] For its part, the United States was strongly disinclined to confront the Russians even in negotiations. Most notably in the Dulles era, we remained unmoved by successive Russian offers to negotiate a European settlement. Occasionally we were dragged, glumly, into discussions at the insistence of our allies. But we preferred, we said, to "negotiate from strength," and we were not yet ready.[2]

By the early 1960s, however, the strong inward-looking tendency toward concentration appeared to be waning if not reversing. For one thing, the progress of consolidation had aroused the inherent contradictions in each of the blocs. The various groupings in the Third World were among the earliest to disintegrate, and in the 1960s, the communist bloc came into serious disarray as the open Sino-Soviet quarrel split the world movement. As the shameful Czech affair demonstrated all too clearly, the Russians still could not maintain their European bloc without the Red Army, even when local communists were in power. But the heavy Russian hand in Prague could not resolve the tension and demoralization throughout the communist world.

The decline of the Atlantic bloc has been less theatrical, although clearly visible. In a sense, the Atlantic bloc has carried the seeds of its own dissolution from the beginning. For, with the active encouragement of American policy, there have been not one, but two blocs in the West—the Atlantic bloc, built around NATO and various economic organizations like the OECD and the IMF, and the European bloc, grouped around the European communities. Each of these two western blocs has had its federalist enthusiasts who have hoped that dynamic concentrating forces would eventually sweep aside national boundaries, and "spill over" into new multinational regional forms. But the Europeanists and Atlanticists had rival contexts in mind, and both have competed for Western Europe.

Nevertheless, for a long time, there was surprisingly little friction between these two congealing western groupings, even if they covered much of the same territory, for each bloc operated primarily in a different sphere. The Atlantic bloc, while it had important economic institutions, was primarily concerned with military defense under a loose American hegemony. The European communities, on the other hand, concerned themselves primarily with continental economic integration, in arrangements within which the Americans were not formally included.* But throughout the 1950s, Americans, flattered by the notion of a European United States, were among the most enthusiastic backers of the Common Market and of the whole European movement that lay behind it. The slogan, "European Unity in Atlantic Partnership" or the various metaphors about dumbbells or pillars seemed enough to pacify any apprehensions over the presence of two rival *foci* for western concentration.

By the 1960s, however, the continental grouping had become a serious economic force, beginning to provoke Washington to a concern about America's own economic interests as well as a more thoughtful view about the European movement's political implications. By 1970 the Common Market's threat to American economic interests was a frequent theme among American econo-

---

* An early major attempt to mix the two spheres, the unfortunate European Defense Community, showed the wisdom of keeping them separate. Essentially a European response to America's insistence on rearming Germany, the EDC enjoyed only mixed approval in Washington. In the EDC's final defeat by the French Assembly in 1954, the biggest losers were probably the European federalists, who had chosen to make their stand around the issue best calculated to arouse a successful nationalist reaction. See Coral Bell, *Negotiation from Strength* (New York, 1963), pp. 60–63; George W. Ball, *The Discipline of Power* (Boston, 1968), pp. 39–56; David Calleo, *Europe's Future: The Grand Alternative* (New York, 1965), pp. 49–51; and Daniel Lerner and Raymond Aron, *France Defeats EDC* (New York, 1957).

mists and government officials. Economic questions had become a major source of European-American discord.

But the western bloc's most serious troubles in the 1960s took place within that sphere in which America was predominant, the military bloc of NATO. Unlike the EEC, NATO was, of course, very much an American creation. The American bureaucratic mind, given a wicked enemy to overcome and a new job to be done, set about with characteristic vigor to build an elaborate structure typical of America's military and diplomatic establishment.

As we have seen, in 1950 the United States assumed the primary initiative for organizing the defense of Europe. An American general of towering prestige became the first Supreme Allied Commander (SACEUR) and organized an interallied staff and supply apparatus of wartime proportions.[3] The Russians, competing even in the proliferation of bureaucracies, organized the Warsaw Pact and Comecon to tie together the dreary and brutal puppet regimes the Red Army imposed on Eastern Europe.[4]

While there was some opposition to becoming an American military protectorate, those Europeans in power, reflecting the general weariness and fear, welcomed the American leadership with open arms.[5] The British, for example, who might presumably have been postwar Europe's natural leaders, threw over their own European defense scheme, the Brussels Pact of 1948, in exchange for NATO. Britain preferred her special partnership in the Atlantic Alliance to the leadership of Europe. Indeed, just as some Americans seemed more Europeanist than the Europeans, many British became more Atlanticist than the Americans.[6] British governments lost whatever enthusiasm they had for European unity and indeed, by 1950, actually refused to join the

Coal and Steel Community.[7] In effect, Britain took herself out of Europe.

In France, de Gaulle grumbled at the dangers of Europe's losing the capacity for independent action, but he was out of power and his prospects for returning were not bright. The Fourth Republic, which was bogged down first in Indochina and then in Algeria, was in no position to take the lead in European defense.[8]

In Germany, the Socialists protested that Adenauer's firm pro-American policy was designed to seal Germany's division in order to secure the western half for the postwar Christian Democratic, Catholic, and capitalist establishment.[9] But for the majority of Germans, after two decades of adventure culminating in defeat, devastation, and shame, Adenauer's friendship with America seemed the best opportunity to climb from the abyss.

Thus Britain, France, and Germany, each in its own way, acquiesced in the formation of the Atlantic military bloc and the consequent consolidation of Europe's partition. Nevertheless, although the Europeans were happy enough to have the American commitment and troops, they showed, as we have seen, great restraint in their own contributions, and they reserved their creative enthusiasm for the European movement, with its promise of a less constricted future. The collective military sphere was given over to America.

The concession seemed natural. For only America held the weapons upon which Europe's defense was generally believed to depend. It was America's nuclear monopoly which gave the United States its hegemonic role in NATO and assured that the defense of Europe would be, in effect, primarily an American rather than a European affair. Nor have successive American governments ever wanted it to be otherwise. American military thinking, whatever its change of fashion, never seriously contemplated anything other than the American nuclear monopoly and hence, in the military sphere, American hegemony and European dependence.*

In the early Eisenhower era, for example, the doctrine of massive retaliation saw Europe's defense hanging almost entirely upon America's strategic deterrent. With the growing Russian nuclear capabilities, American military thinking turned toward tactical nuclear weapons on the battlefield. Western Europe was endowed with seven thousand atomic weapons, all supplied and all ultimately controlled by the Americans. By the 1960s a fresh appraisal jolted the American military thinking into the new doctrine of flexible response.[10] But the new doctrine, despite its emphasis on conventional defense, suggested not a decrease, but actually an increase in America's hegemonic position. Since the Americans controlled the higher reaches of nuclear violence, it was said, they should control the whole range of force to prevent confrontations from "escalating and uncontrollably becoming irrational."[11]

In summary, whatever the changes in NATO's decoration, the architectural pattern has remained hegemonic. So monolithic a style is not to everyone's taste. In particular, it has gradually lost its appeal to the major European powers themselves. As a result, Britain and France, each in its own fashion, have taken their distance from America's nuclear hegemony in NATO, while Germany has grown increasingly restive within it.

---

* The Multilateral Nuclear Force (MLF) scheme sought to provide the illusion of participation without the substance of control. More recent attempts to increase European consultation in strategic planning, while helpful, do not essentially alter America's nuclear hegemony. See Thomas C. Wiegele, "The Origins of the MLF Concept, 1957–60," *Orbis*, Fall 1968.

Essentially, the tensions between America and her principal NATO allies revolve around two basic issues: proliferation and détente.

Neither Britain nor France could be expected to feel at home in a bipolar world system that placed them under the military hegemony of the United States. Their resistance to this fate forms a major subplot within the drama of Atlantic and European concentration. First Britain in 1952 and then France in 1960 produced their own nuclear weapons. Both sought thereby not so much to dissociate themselves from the Alliance as to gain a special status within it. The British were immediately successful. Since they had initiated us into nuclear weapons technology, we felt constrained to admit them to a nuclear special relationship, even if the arrangement clearly contradicted the hegemonic logic of NATO. The contradiction became clear as the French also developed nuclear weapons and we refused to extend them a similar accommodation.[12]

With the Nassau agreements in 1962, we hoped to accommodate both Britain and France. The British were assuaged, but the French, unimpressed, continued working on the independent nuclear force which we have opposed. By 1966 the French walked out of NATO's military organization.

The tensions between France, Britain, and the United States have been self-defeating all around. The quarrels both undermined NATO and made it difficult to create any European substitute. As seems usual in this century, Britain and France, to their mutual cost, have managed to defeat each other. Meanwhile, the United States has become more firmly harnessed to Europe's defense than ever.

German diffidence toward a permanent hegemonic nuclear pattern became evident in the widespread resistance to the Nonproliferation Treaty. Germans have turned from America's Atlantic hegemony less as a result of reviving aspirations to great power status than from fear of being caught in the toils of a Soviet-American entente negotiated at Germany's expense. In the earlier Adenauer era, the Germans, despairing of any reasonable response from the Russians, were contented enough to wait for better days under the cover of America's nuclear and diplomatic hegemony. German restiveness dates from the early 1960s, when it became apparent that the Cold War might thaw into a broad Soviet-American understanding—a development that presented Europe in general and Germany in particular not only with new opportunities, but also new risks.[13]

Along with transatlantic economic tensions and the military issues arising over nuclear control, détente has constituted the second major disrupting issue in the Atlantic bloc. The problems are not new. From the early 1950s there has been an intermittent current of conciliation between Russia and the United States, often interrupted by particular issues and opportunities, but nevertheless steadily renewed. The causes are easily understood. The superpowers have several interests in common. Neither wants a nuclear war or nuclear proliferation. Both are overextended and conservative. Neither is seriously displeased with the status quo. The Russians, like the Americans, have their own particular reasons for wanting détente. Economic goals continue to suggest domestic relaxation and liberalization. Satellite unrest and the growing Sino-Soviet quarrel suggest the advantages of a more stable and comfortable relationship with the West.

Nevertheless, as we have discovered in NATO, the conciliation of blocs at the top promotes their disintegration at the bottom. In other words, as world concentration has reached its fullest logic, it has simultaneously begun its decline. The progress of détente, while it reveals the harmonies of interest among the superpowers, also exposes the conflicts of interest within each of their blocs. If the United States and Russia see in détente a way to preserve the world of their blocs, their allies look for a way to escape from hegemony.

Détente between the superpowers can be seen as the prelude to two possible outcomes: disengagement or condominium.

A policy aimed at disengagement would seek stable political settlements in regions of confrontation, settlements satisfying not only the superpowers, but the major local powers as well. The guiding principles of a settlement would be national self-determination and regional interdependence and balance. Boundaries would be drawn to produce politically and economically viable states, related together in a stable system of natural balances and explicit guarantees, designed to give the whole a certain solidarity against outside intervention. Unnecessary barriers to normal trade and communications within the region would be minimal.

In Europe, such a settlement demands the resolution of the German problem in a way accepted by both Germanys, their neighbors, and the two superpowers. It would probably mean some kind of German confederation, partially disarmed and inspected, along with a Western European military and political grouping as a firm if not hostile counterweight to Russian power. The western grouping would presumably be allied to the United States, but not integrated under American military hegemony. Eastern Europe would be allied militarily to Russia, but allowed a wider band of domestic freedom and economic openness.

With such a resolution, the superpowers could withdraw from their military confrontation across the middle of Germany. The resultant situation would ideally be stable and self-sustaining, neither a threat to peace in the world, nor an irresistible temptation to outside intervention.

A policy aimed at condominium would obviously seek a different pattern for world order. The superpowers would concede spheres of influence to each other and agree to cooperate and preserve the status quo, even at the expense of their allies. In Europe, America and Russia would decide that half the continent was better than none, that the larger interests of world stability forbade the lesser goal of European unification and independence —developments which might, after all, release uncontrolled energies and arouse widespread uncertainty and fear. Various concessions might be made to the interests and illusions of the lesser powers, but the reality of condominium would be sustained. There are, of course, several variations on these models—a number of them discussed in the chapters to follow.[14] But it should be clear, at this point, why détente has been a major cause of friction within the western alliance.

In pursuing détente with the Soviet Union, American policy has often given the appearance of preferring condominium to disengagement. De Gaulle exaggerated our conscious pursuit of condominium. But our principal European initiatives in the 1960s, it must be confessed, mostly tried to consolidate our own bloc rather than to end Europe's division. To be sure, we have a formula that is supposed to make it possible to pursue both aims simultaneously. We still argue that a strong NATO is the best way to force Europe's reunification. But since we have long abandoned any serious intention of using western military strength to exploit divisions in the eastern camp, the old notion of a tightly integrated NATO, bargaining over Europe from a position of strength, does not make much sense, and neither does the equally venerable formula of hanging on together to wait for the Russians to collapse. As we ourselves ardently pursue friendly agreement with Russia, the supposedly continuing Soviet menace seems a less and less compelling reason for our allies to remain huddled together, rusticated in the NATO fortress, while its absent commander has suspiciously frequent and lingering visits with the enemy.

To be fair, we have not tried to stop our allies from pursuing their own arrangements with the Soviet bloc. But while we have shown uneasy tolerance for German and Gaullist *Ostpolitik*, we have ourselves contributed remarkably little in the way of new ideas or policies for a European settlement that would eliminate the divisions of the Cold War. We were, for example, mute before the tragedy of Czechoslovakia. Afterward, our principal recommendations called for strengthening the German forces of NATO. There was little thought of how the Russians might be eased out of their unhappy predicament in Eastern Europe through a broad European settlement.*

And while we have been discouraging NATO from responding to Warsaw Pact offers of negotiation, we

---

* Some felt that the Czech invasion offered a good opportunity to sound out the seriousness of the continual offers from the East for a security conference and, in particular, for an inspected nuclear free zone in Central Europe. If, as the Russians loudly proclaimed, the invasion had been predicated on subversive German influence in Czechoslovakia, a dramatic offer to deal with the supposed military threat would have reduced Russia's motives or excuses for intervention. If, on the other hand, the Russian action was based on fears of spreading liberalism within the communist world, the United States would have isolated more convincingly the cause of Russian actions, and exonerated herself from the charges of tacit complicity, which arose inevitably from her failure to take any action at all.

have ourselves actively been pursuing bilateral understandings with the Soviets, sometimes, as with the Nonproliferation Treaty, along lines that seem blatantly unconcerned with the interests of our allies. While we have pursued the bilateral SALT talks with relative eagerness and close attention to the issues, we have shown little inclination to commit ourselves to a European security conference, or indeed, for a long time, even to begin thinking about it seriously.

In short, our allies may be forgiven for suspecting that we do not find the present European situation uncomfortable and have not given very serious thought to changing it. Indeed, they might even be forgiven for believing that, if they left the management of their diplomatic affairs entirely to the United States, the two blocs that divide Europe might last a very long time. It is not surprising that the revisionists in Europe are more inclined to take their distance from the Atlantic bloc. Thus the détente that was meant to complete Atlantic integration in fact threatens to destroy it.

As the 1960s unfolded, all these inherent tensions began to trouble the dream of Atlantica. The elements for a European revolt were at hand. De Gaulle brought the spark. Thanks to the French, and the Vietnamese, the American imagination has at last begun to paint a new picture of the world.

V. THE GAULLIST CHALLENGE

In the 1960s it was France and China who were the principal rebels against the world of blocs. Both are great and arrogant nations, once predominant in their own spheres and now fallen on hard times. Both have been led in the present era by revolutionary autocrats, world-historical figures larger than life. China, of course, is vastly larger—a potential superpower in her own right. But France, if small, has also been agile, a considerable asset in a world of myopic dinosaurs. In diplomacy, as in physics, levers adroitly applied can replace brute strength. Not infrequently, de Gaulle was able to demonstrate the multiplier effects of intelligence.

Perhaps the best epitaph for de Gaulle's political career can be found, appropriately enough, in his own *Memoirs*:

... I asked myself if among all those who spoke of revolution, I was not, in truth, the only revolutionary.[1]

De Gaulle has always seemed happiest in rebellion. In the end, he half-wanted to join the barricades against his own regime. Like Mao, he was bored with his own middle-aged revolution.

The world has known many Don Quixotes, but few who have succeeded so well. Gaullist grandeur has generally included a streak of cold prudence. If he convinced himself that he was Joan of Arc, he taught his enemies that he was Richelieu. He learned his diplomacy, not from the grandiose schemes of Napoleon, but from the prudent calculations of Talleyrand.*

---

* Charles de Gaulle's summation of Napoleon's career: "Tragic revenge of measure; just wrath of reason; but superhuman prestige and marvelous valor of arms." *La France et Son Armée* (Paris, 1938), p. 150.

De Gaulle's most important enemy was Franklin Delano Roosevelt. It is against the shade of Roosevelt that de Gaulle has been struggling all these years. For Roosevelt was the architect of the world system which de Gaulle dedicated his life to dismantling.

Franklin Roosevelt was governed by the loftiest ambitions. His intelligence, his knowledge and his audacity gave him the ability, the powerful state of which he was the leader afforded him the means, and the war offered him the occasion to realize them. If the great nation he directed had long been inclined to isolate itself from distant enterprises and to mistrust a Europe ceaselessly lacerated by wars and revolutions, a kind of messianic impulse now swelled the American spirit and oriented it toward vast undertakings. The United States, delighting in her resources, feeling that she no longer had within herself sufficient scope for her energies, wishing to help those who were in misery or bondage the world over, yielded in her turn to that taste for intervention in which the instinct for domination cloaked itself. It was precisely this tendency that President Roosevelt espoused. He has therefore done everything to enable his country to take part in the world conflict. He was now fulfilling his destiny, impelled as he was by the secret admonition of death.[2]

De Gaulle's account of their final confrontation is worth remembering:

"It is the West," I told President Roosevelt, "that must be restored. If it regains its balance, the rest of the world, whether it wishes or not, will take it for an example. If it declines, barbarism will ultimately sweep everything away. Western Europe, despite its dissensions and its distress, is essential to the West. Nothing can replace the value, the power, the shining examples of these ancient peoples. This is true of France above all, which of all the great nations of Europe is the only one which was, is and always will be your ally. I know you are preparing to aid France materially, and that aid will be invaluable to her. But it is in the political realm that she must recover her vigor, her self-reliance and, consequently, her role. How can she do this if she is excluded from the organization of the great world powers and their decisions, if she loses her African and Asian territories

—in short, if the settlement of the war definitively imposes upon her the psychology of the vanquished?"

Roosevelt avowed his affection for France, but:

As for the future, he was anything but convinced of the re-birth and renewal of our regime. With bitterness he described what his feelings were when before the war he watched the spectacle of our political impotence unfold before his eyes. "Even I, the President of the United States," he told me, "would some-times find myself incapable of remembering the name of the current head of the French government. For the moment, you are there, and you see with what kind attentions my country welcomes you. But will you be there at the tragedy's end?"

De Gaulle reflects in his *Memoirs:*

The American President's remarks ultimately proved to me that, in foreign affairs, logic and sentiment do not weigh heavily in comparison with the realities of power; that what matters is what one takes and what one can hold on to; that to regain her place, France must count only on herself. I told him this. He smiled and concluded: "We shall do what we can. But it is true that to serve France no one can replace the French people."[3]

As de Gaulle saw it, Roosevelt's grandiose ambitions led Europe directly to catastrophe at Yalta. There, the Anglo-Saxons presumed to settle Europe's future in France's absence, and the result was a divided continent of two blocs, each dominated by a rival and alien he-gemony. De Gaulle's entire diplomatic campaign, as he himself saw it, aimed at dismantling the blocs and re-storing a self-sustaining European system, within which France would play a principal role. De Gaulle's ideal was not the anti-Russian Atlantica (an Americanized Europe from Honolulu to Hamburg) but a European Europe from the Atlantic to the Urals.

De Gaulle's European vision inevitably puzzles those who forget that the world existed before 1945. His ideal Europe was to be neither an intense federation ruled from Brussels nor an imperium directed from Moscow, but an interdependent state system, governed by balances simultaneously limiting the ambitions and securing the safety of each—a system ensuring that "each in particular, if convinced of his superiority, does not aspire to omnipotence."[4]

De Gaulle has tried to be a modern Talleyrand, seeking to restore the balanced system shattered by Hitler's Napoleonic drive for hegemony. Ironically, de Gaulle's vision was inspired by his strong feeling for the interdependence of the European nations. For him, Germany's unmeasured ambition and ruin graphically illustrated that interdependence. After their orgy of self-laceration, victors and losers alike in Europe found themselves protectorates and dependencies of outsiders. Wise statesmanship, de Gaulle believed, had to extricate Europe from its alien guardians and, by restoring a balanced European community, exile Russia and America to the fringes where they belonged.

De Gaulle's preoccupations doubtless owed something to his wartime quarrels and humiliations. But his policies were natural to any strong government in France and, for that reason alone, are likely to survive their author.* For it is only natural that the middle powers of Europe should seek escape from duopoly. And it is only natural that France should lead the revisionists within the western camp.

* For a discussion of the widespread domestic support enjoyed by Gaullist foreign policy, see Stanley Hoffmann, *Gulliver's Troubles* (New York, 1968), pp. 415–16. It could also be argued that the differences between the foreign policies of the Fourth and Fifth Republics were more of style than of substance. The Fourth Republic, by strongly supporting European unity built around Franco-German rapprochement might be called equally, and perhaps more effectively, revisionist than the Fifth.

Among the prewar great powers, France, after Germany, suffered the greatest loss of status and prestige from the war. And the postwar Atlantic Alliance offered France, among all the Europeans, the least chance to recoup. France's dim prospects could be blamed partly on America's refusal to take the French seriously. While the British could find consolation in an Anglo-American special relation, institutionalized in the nuclear and intelligence liaisons, the French were denied nuclear partnership and felt themselves unsupported in their costly and humiliating colonial wars.[5] As we have seen, nothing illustrated better the low estate of the French military in NATO than the parceling out of top commands—seven for the Americans, five for the British, and one for the French. So much for Marshal Foch!

Even defeated Germany had more favorable relations with Washington. For Adenauer, the United States was not only his disarmed country's military protector, but NATO was the route to regaining national independence and respectability. For the United States, German arms were needed in NATO to sustain the European confrontation with Russia. Adenauer could and did bargain skillfully to regain Germany's freedom of action in return for her soldiers. For the time being, at least, it was in Germany's interest that the Cold War should continue. It allowed the Federal Republic to regain its sovereignty and meanwhile prevented a Soviet-American settlement at Germany's expense.

France, on the other hand, got little from the Cold War and the western bloc. Any such grouping that includes Germany but leaves out Russia puts France at a particular disadvantage. Russia was France's traditional ally against the German colossus. Indeed, after 1870, France's continuation as a major independent power in relation to Germany depended on a Russian alliance.

The isolation of Russia from the West after World War I greatly reduced French security. That Britain was no substitute was the lesson of the 1930s and the French were unlikely to forget it. Neither was America a satisfactory substitute. A Franco-American alliance, without a corresponding Franco-Russian alliance for insurance, did not so much increase French power as drown it. In short, a return to traditional relations with Russia was essential to the revival of French power. Hence there was interested hope as well as lofty judgment in de Gaulle's view on ideology: "In the ceaseless movement of the world, all doctrines, all schools, all rebellions have only one time. Communism will pass. But France will not pass."[6]

De Gaulle's attempt to thaw the blocs involved a far-reaching and supple strategy operating on several levels. France attacked America's military hegemony in NATO and in 1966 withdrew from it. Meanwhile, France promoted European solidarity against the threatening American economic preponderance and conducted an elaborate campaign with Bonn, Moscow, and Washington itself to entice all three into creating a new European order.

The withdrawal from NATO was perhaps the single most spectacular initiative. Of course, France's geographical insulation made it easy enough to renounce American protection while continuing to enjoy it. But the French went further and promoted a military doctrine which both challenged the long-range adequacy of America's hegemonic military protection and pointed to a European alternative.

Compared to the elegant permutations of America's new flexible response doctrine, the French strategic argument was simple and plausible. Both the American and the French doctrines began with the same assumption:

After Sputnik, America was going to be vulnerable at home and her nuclear deterrent in Europe therefore less effective.

The American doctrine called for more European conventional options to space out any confrontation and deny the Russians easy success at any level. Moreover, in so delicate a game of mutual calculation, it was essential, we insisted, that decision making be even more centralized in Washington.

French military thinkers concluded, not that Europeans should provide more conventional options for America, but that they should provide a nuclear option for themselves. "Deterrence" would be thereby increased. The Russians would be less likely to gamble on a supine reaction to an invasion of Europe if Europeans, as well as their American allies, had independent nuclear forces. True, these European nuclear forces would be small, but nevertheless, according to French military doctrine, small deterrents could be effective. Double uncertainty would raise the risks and thus enhance deterrence. Merely increasing European conventional strength, as the Americans wanted, would suggest an unwillingness to use nuclear weapons and actually decrease deterrence.[7]

Official American experts found these conclusions unsound, involving costly duplications in "Atlantic" defense, and introducing dangerously complicating factors in the orderly "management" of crises. The American conclusions were transparently self-interested. European national deterrants might precipitate a nuclear war without our assent, and the Russians, having been devastated in their own homeland by Europeans, might see no reason to spare the United States. But, we argued, whereas general harm would result from a European proliferation, no harm could come to Europe from leaving us with the nuclear monopoly. Europe was more than adequately protected by our deterrent. Even if the Russians suspected our willingness to commit suicide for someone else, the uncertainty would be so great, and the cost of miscalculation so enormous, that they would never dare to call our bluff.

In any event, we were hoping to develop an over-all understanding with the Russians. Neither superpower wanted to drift helplessly into suicide. We suspected that for their crisis managers, as well as our own, the ideal world would have America and Russia the only nuclear powers, closely in touch with each other, mutually interested in stability, each controlling its bloc, and both cooperating to prevent proliferation. European nuclear forces reduced the prospects for any such stable nuclear duopoly.[8]

Of course it was precisely this superpower entente to preserve the status quo in Europe, this new Yalta, which de Gaulle was hoping to prevent. To do so, according to de Gaulle, Europe needed to keep open its own nuclear options.

Taken thus far, de Gaulle's military arguments had considerable force. On the other hand, even if the planned French nuclear force might come to have considerable military potential, no one else in Europe would be likely to renounce the enormous American nuclear force for a small French one. But there is little evidence that de Gaulle had such a development in mind. While the French might be interested in a European military coalition which would take over from the Americans the primary responsibility for organizing European defense, de Gaulle nevertheless admitted that Europe would need and want, for any foreseeable future, an American alliance as insurance against Russian aggression. All the same, as the General never tired of saying, America and

Europe had distinct interests, and the American hegemony of NATO was not designed to safeguard those distinct European interests. NATO's hegemonic grip had to be broken, de Gaulle believed, before Western Europe could evolve from a protectorate that could be taken for granted into an independent ally whose interests could not be sacrificed for the sake of a Soviet-American duopoly. A stronger and more militarily self-reliant Europe would be in a better position to cultivate Russia as a counterbalance to excessively domineering pressures from America, while nevertheless maintaining a transatlantic alliance against Russian pretensions to European hegemony. In the Gaullist view, every balance has two sides.

Along with their attack on America's military hegemony in NATO, the French have tried to rally a European bloc to define and assert collective European economic interests, especially in the trade and monetary fields. France, for example, promoted a tough European position in the Kennedy Round. Most notably, the French have demanded a fundamental revision of the postwar monetary system. The monetary system, in de Gaulle's view, has not been "objective." It has allowed the United States and Britain, because the dollar and the pound are reserve currencies, to run deficits as they please, and, in effect, has forced the Europeans to finance them.[9] The French have also been leaders in the protest against the americanization of European business.

While de Gaulle sought to make himself the spokesman for Europe's interests as a bloc distinct from the United States, he was never popular with the federalist "good" Europeans. According to the standard Europeanist view, even if the French under de Gaulle may have been more committed to European independence than any other government, their actions have actually worked against European self-determination. Indeed, it has often been said, Gaullist France has followed a contradictory and destructive policy. Self-determination for Europe requires a federal state with resources on the scale of the United States and Russia. France, by cutting down the supranational institutions of Brussels, has made European union and hence independence less likely than ever.

De Gaulle, for his part, always scorned these full-blown federalist arguments. Europe's liberation, he argued, can only be achieved through the lead given by a strong, independent, and determined government, devoted to Europe's broader interests and capable of outwitting and defying the superpowers. No federal government of Western Europe could give such a lead. Such a government would necessarily include so many diverse interests and have so feeble a hold on popular allegiance that it would inevitably be disunited, weak, pliable, and permanently subordinate to America. A France swallowed up in a European dinosaur would be as helpless as the rest.

Occasionally, of course, de Gaulle pushed his own plan for a European confederal structure, the Europe of States of the Fouchet Plan.[10] But here his initiatives foundered on the issue of British participation. Britain, de Gaulle argued, was still Atlantic in her perspectives and hence basically opposed to building a European bloc distinct from America. To admit so willful and powerful a state into the councils of the Six, by destroying what tenuous unity did exist, would only ensure the paralysis of common action.[11] The logic of things, de Gaulle was careful to admit, might eventually change Britain's orientation, and near the end, he began to explore British interest in more intimate collaboration, perhaps in the military field. The result must have been dismaying, but Pompidou's regime, partially dissociated from years of bad relations, may find the British more receptive.

In many respects, de Gaulle's views on European integration are commonsensical and scarcely seem to justify the fanatical opprobrium they have earned among the "good" Europeans. Nevertheless, de Gaulle's policy toward building a European community, even if based on sound enough principles, was hardly an unqualified success. But it is hard to believe, in retrospect, that he expected or even wanted more than he achieved. He sought to promote European solidarity on many issues, and to make a success of the Common Market, especially when it was to France's economic interests to do so. But he had no real interest, at the stage where he was, for building any elaborate European machinery which might constrict his wider diplomatic initiatives—policies essential, he believed, to breaking the Cold War deadlock. Above all, he had no desire to promote a tight Western European grouping, internally preoccupied and externally inert, which would only complicate the process of a larger European reunification. He preferred a France unfettered in her revisionist initiatives by the need for achieving consensus among a half dozen or more heterogeneous partners. To be sure, the General probably found this independence as congenial to himself as he believed it was necessary for Europe.

In any event, under de Gaulle the French gave an ample demonstration of the uses to which independence might be put. Although he took great interest in the Third World and the Eastern European satellites, the grand campaign against the blocs focused on Bonn, Moscow, and Washington.

The campaign in Bonn began in the early 1960s.[12] Thanks to the earlier enlightened policies of Adenauer and the Fourth Republic, there was already a conscious sense of French-German entente, which has been, in fact, the basis for the European Communities. With de Gaulle the friendship became more adventurous and troubled. The General aimed to woo the Germans away from their close dependence on the United States and to encourage them in a more active and conciliatory policy toward détente. His initial success was striking, but transitory, as the Americans were aroused and the ancient and suddenly rambunctious Adenauer was replaced by the more docile Erhard. Nevertheless, Gaullist ideas played a considerable role in subsequently dislodging Erhard and in promoting the Great Coalition and its *Ostpolitik*.

Adenauer's postwar policy had avoided direct dealing with the Russians on reunification, and it had taken every opportunity to bind the Federal Republic into the West, while bargaining shrewdly to get free of the special disabilities imposed by defeat. Adenauer probably proceeded on the broad assumption that, for the foreseeable future, reunification could only be bought at what was for him an unacceptable price—a Germany dependent on Russia, disarmed, neutral, and socialist, if not communist. It seemed much better to work for a restored and rearmed West Germany, its democratic institutions consolidated and its ties with the West irrevocable, a strong half-Germany which would, Adenauer reckoned, be in a far better position ultimately to deal with the Soviets.[13]

De Gaulle pointed out to the Germans that time was marching on. Absorption into the Atlantic bloc, while it might give Germany protection and respectability, offered no prospect for reunification, and Russia would never withdraw her iron grip from Eastern Europe as long as

Western Europe was a forward outpost of American military power. The progress of détente, and the special interest of the Kennedy administration in coming to terms with Russia, greatly increased the danger of a direct agreement between the superpowers to stabilize their positions, essentially at Germany's expense.

While West Germany could not now break with America, the Gaullist argument ran, she should take her distance and back off from an inflexible Cold War position. While not recognizing East Germany, she should recognize the Oder-Neisse boundaries and seek closer economic and political relations with Russia and with Eastern Europe.

Germany's advances to the East, de Gaulle argued, should be in broad partnership with France, for France, unlike the United States, shared with Germany a fundamental interest in unifying Europe and banishing the hegemonies. A Germany acting without France would arouse the older specter of German *Mitteleuropa*—and excite defensive instincts among the Russians and the other Eastern Europeans.*

While collaboration between Bonn and Paris has not been as close as the French might have hoped, Germany nevertheless transformed herself in the 1960s from a docile protectorate into a revisionist power, a develop-

---

* Paris was said to be irritated over the enthusiasm of German economic interests for close relations with Czechoslovakia before the Soviet intervention. During his visit in Bonn, de Gaulle allegedly "told stunned German officials that Bonn was in part to blame for the Czechoslovak crisis because it had asserted its economic power in Prague and had given rise to Soviet fears that the Czechoslovaks might break out of the Warsaw Pact." *New York Times*, October 3, 1968. The French President "came close to adopting the Soviet argument," the *Times* reported on October 6, 1968, and he asserted "that Bonn should leave 'Eastern policy' solely to Paris." The account possibly exaggerates, but there was considerable friction.

ment that not only hastens the dissolution of the Atlantic bloc, and impairs a superpower deal, but also strengthens France's hand with the Russians. At the same time, Germany's more conciliatory policy toward Eastern Europe has increased the strains within the communist bloc and thereby increased the cost to Russia of maintaining her tight hegemony.

But while de Gaulle caused trouble for the Russians, he was eager to cultivate them as well, among other reasons to make clear to Moscow that America and Western Europe were not synonymous. De Gaulle's demonstrated ability to disrupt the Atlantic bloc made him difficult to ignore in the Kremlin despite irritation at his unsettling machinations in Germany and Eastern Europe. Thus de Gaulle used the rivalry of superpowers to prevent their condominium, and indeed, deflected the force of that rivalry toward the disruption of the blocs themselves.

While doing his best to undermine the Soviet bloc, de Gaulle simultaneously tried to persuade the Russians of the advantages for them of a joint superpower disengagement from Europe. It would point, he believed, to his celebrated "Europe from the Atlantic to the Urals." There would evolve a Western European grouping, no longer dominated by the United States, with Germany united in a loose federation and without nuclear weapons. Such a grouping would pose no threat to Russia, and would permit a corresponding Russian relaxation in Eastern Europe. Even if that area remained a loose military protectorate of the Russians, with the Central European superpower confrontation ended, the Soviets could permit their neighbors and perhaps themselves much more domestic liberty and international intercourse. De Gaulle's European system would give Russia a far more relaxed and stable western frontier, and free her energies for domestic growth and Asian problems.*

The system was to be sustained by an elaborate series of power balances and at least tacit reinsurance treaties. For example, while loyally pleading the necessity of Germany's unification for any stable European system, de Gaulle no doubt also reminded the Russians of the traditional Franco-Russian interest in containing German exuberance. Thus, the explicit Franco-German alliance to balance Russia would have a tacit Franco-Russian understanding about Germany. Similarly the loose alliance between Western Europe and America against Russia would be conditioned by a similar understanding with Russia should America attempt to reassert a tight European hegemony. A balance-of-power system, qualified by all these conditions, becomes, in effect, a kind of general "security system." It is not so much the alliance of one group against another, but a general agreement to prevent any one power from dominating the others.[14]

While de Gaulle's vision called for the retirement of the superpowers from the exercise of their present active power in mutual confrontation across Central Europe, it nevertheless presupposed their continuing potential power to guarantee and stabilize the European system as a whole. Russia would be needed to limit both Germany and the United States. On the other hand, without

* De Gaulle was among the first to draw hopeful conclusions for a European settlement from the Chinese-Russian quarrel. French recognition of China came in late January 1964, after the open break between China and Russia in July 1963: ". . . in Asia, where the frontier between the two states, from the Hindu Kush to Vladivostok, is the longest that exists in the world, Russia's interest, which is to conserve and maintain, and China's, which is to grow and to acquire, cannot be considered identical." De Gaulle, Press Conference, January 31, 1964.

the United States in the background, Russia would soon menace both France and Germany. De Gaulle wanted the United States to abdicate hegemony, but not to withdraw its presence altogether.

De Gaulle did his best to make the existing hegemonic bloc system intolerable for Americans and Russians alike and to suggest a pleasing alternative. The Johnson administration focused almost exclusively on the disruptive aspect of Gaullist policy and ignored the constructive possibilities it suggested. The disruptions, to be sure, were difficult to ignore.

In the mid-1960s de Gaulle made himself the Terrible Old Man of the West. He withdrew from NATO's machinery and threw it out of France, publicly called the American role in Vietnam "detestable,"[15] and attacked the dollar. The three attacks had one aspect in common: they were all directed against the outlines of world duopoly. By the late 1960s the General, suspecting that Washington was weary of its visions of duopoly and at last receptive to schemes for disengagement, began a new campaign of smiles.

The French have tried, in a variety of ways, to demonstrate to Washington the practical usefulness of independent, medium-sized powers in preserving general world order, particularly in situations where the rival superpowers are muscle-bound. Thus French diplomacy has sought to play a mediating role in the Middle East and, no doubt, would like to do so in Vietnam, should the portents ever be favorable. De Gaulle's outspoken criticism of America in Vietnam gives France all the more leverage and makes her all the more valuable to America as a potential mediator. The French point out the useful role they play in Africa, where their large aid program sustains new states which might otherwise be yet another cause for concern and expense to the American government.

The Gaullist demarche has tried to point out to the American imagination the advantages not only of European disengagement, but of a more differentiated international system generally. The world would not collapse, the French suggest, if Washington had a good night's rest. The General even went so far as to court the sour British and suggest a new western military and economic grouping.*

The Pompidou government is continuing the campaign of conciliation that began in the last stage of de Gaulle's leadership. But there is little sign that the French have abandoned their revisionist stance, whatever compromises they may have to make with current necessities. For de Gaulle's European vision sprang from abiding French national interests, and any strong French government is likely to remain Gaullist in these matters.[16]

It is an ungenerous spirit that can find nothing to admire in the sweep and finesse of French diplomacy. The French are only a middle power. They cannot destroy the world several times over with their nuclear arsenal. They do not have many aces in their hand, but they

---

* This is known as the Soames Affair, named after the British ambassador to Paris, Christopher Soames. In a meeting with Soames in May 1969, de Gaulle expressed his familiar view that British entry would result in a much looser EEC than had been contemplated. He suggested the British and French begin talking seriously about what the economic and military arrangements for this new Europe should be. The British, ostensibly fearing a Gaullist trap to compromise them with their continental allies, revealed the interview in tones which made clear that their virtue had remained impregnable. The French officially remained unruffled. British handling of the affair was not widely admired. The best comment was perhaps that of former Prime Minister Sir Alec Douglas-Home: The government had "underestimated the resources of diplomacy." *The Times* (London, February 26, 1969).

play their cards very well. If grandeur depends on vision, skill, and pluck rather than size, they are a great nation still.

In any event, in the decade of Gaullist ascendancy, the French have been the principal political power in Western Europe. They have set in motion revisionist ideas and forces which may quite possibly bring down that post-Yalta world of the blocs. De Gaulle's fall may even hasten the process. French leadership will be easier to accept when it is reduced to a more human scale. The General may not live to see his new world unfold, but then victory in these matters is always somewhat banal. In any event the struggle has been glorious enough. The General will be welcomed with full honors by the shades of Richelieu and Talleyrand.

VI. THE INSTABILITY OF THE STATUS QUO: THE MONETARY DIMENSION

Discussions about our European policy often assume that, whereas changes in our transatlantic relationship might be risky, continuing the status quo is not only possible, but relatively safe. Why then press for change? In this view, the settlement that emerged from World War II is more like Vienna in 1815 than Versailles in 1918. Even if many Europeans are unenthusiastic and many of their grievances remain unrequited, the postwar order is nevertheless stable. Unhappy forces seethe, and there are occasional revolutionary eruptions, but in the end they can be contained. For the blocs have tacitly become accepted. Even the dissatisfied are not intolerably uncomfortable, at least in the West, and those powers strong enough to alter things have a common interest in preserving them. Hence in Paris, Bonn, Prague, or Budapest revisionism can be kept within bounds that do not threaten the postwar duopoly.

This comfortable assumption is very likely wrong, even if short-range trends in recent years may seem to confirm it. For a number of rather fundamental political, economic, and strategic factors seem to urge change and steadily raise the costs of American immobility. With such forces at work, a radical reordering of European and transatlantic relationships, while scarcely inevitable, is nevertheless no longer improbable. To develop this point further it is necessary to review the broad evolution of events and forces which control the present situation and threaten the status quo.

To begin with the military alliance itself: By the mid-1960s, the drive toward concentration in the Atlantic Alliance was obviously reversed, and the centrifugal forces of disintegration were clearly gaining. The French withdrawal in 1966 was only one in a series of developments suggesting that NATO's days were numbered, even if the United States continued its fervent support of the status quo. The serious weakness of the dollar, the widespread unpopularity of the Vietnam War, and the apparent progress of a European détente all produced impatience with American leadership and a diffidence toward the Atlantic bloc. A sense of irrelevance began to penetrate even to the busy NATO bureaucracy itself.

To be sure, the immediate effect of the French withdrawal was rather exhilarating at SHAPE. At last there was a real threat. With commendable agility, the entire bureaucratic establishment moved itself intact to Belgium, although the huge logistical and communications network had to be abandoned and was not restored.[1]

Once the unaccustomed excitement of moving was over, however, it was clear that all was not well. With France wandering and Germany increasingly bemused by *Ostpolitik*, NATO felt the need for some serious new initiative to demonstrate its relevance to a world of European détente. As one high official used to say, NATO had to get itself into the "détente management business." Indeed, Atlanticist reformers had argued for years that NATO could be saved from decay only by broadening its scope. The regional military focus was too narrow to sustain interest and commitment. Reformers commonly suggested using NATO's political apparatus to concert western diplomatic strategies beyond the treaty area.[2]

In late 1966 the NATO Council launched the

"Harmel Exercise," a year-long study on the prospects and problems of extending the scope of NATO's collaboration.[3]

It would hardly be fair to describe the Harmel Exercise as unimportant, let alone a failure. It demonstrated the deep reservoir of mutual goodwill that could still be tapped by civilized diplomacy. The French participated along with the others, and there was much useful discussion *in camera*. Quiet talking improved the general mood and doubtless eliminated some unnecessary misunderstanding. In the end, there emerged a general affirmation of the Alliance as a "dynamic and vigorous organization" whose future tasks could be handled within the treaty's framework "by building on the methods and procedures which have proved their value over many years." This was heartening, but vague. The ship could keep afloat, but with very little cargo. The advanced hopes of reformers were disappointed once more. The Council was not about to become the political center for a cohesive Atlantic bloc. Even in its measure of success, the Harmel Exercise pointed up the limitations of the NATO Council and the depth of differences in the Alliance.

None of this should have been surprising. To begin with, the NATO machinery is extraordinarily clumsy for serious discussion. A Council of ambassadors from fifteen heterogeneous nations is an improbable body to hammer out policies or indeed even to consult about them. No doubt a small directory might prove more functional.[4] But finally, disharmony is not so much an accident of faulty machinery for consultation as it is the inevitable result of the differing perceptions of interest among the partners.

As I have argued in Chapter IV, there are, at bottom, two great differences in the Alliance. Together, they mean that NATO cannot become the nascent transatlantic federation dreamed of by the Atlanticists. Meanwhile, the attempt to continue our relationship in so tight a frame as NATO inhibits that integration among the Europeans themselves which is far more in our real interest than the formal continuation of NATO.

It would be well to review these national differences which make NATO's advanced pretensions so unrealistic. One major difference turns around the opposing approaches to military strategy, the other around distinct national approaches to détente.

The military argument has already been discussed. As the Russians acquired the unquestioned ability to devastate a large part of the United States in any general nuclear exchange, both the British and then the French built independent nuclear forces and argued that their own national defense should not depend entirely on the credibility of America's willingness to die for Europe. And to be taken seriously by the superpowers, both European countries felt the need for a nuclear passport.

The American response to growing vulnerability has been equally understandable. No conflict in Europe, we hoped, would spread to engulf our cities in a massive nuclear exchange. We embraced the doctrine of flexible response, designed to contain any Russian military adventures in Europe, if possible without resorting to nuclear weapons. The new doctrine encouraged a build-up of conventional forces. If nuclear weapons were ever necessary, it was hoped that their use could be limited to the tactical battle area, that is to say, Western Europe rather than the United States. The American government, responsibly enough, was trying to broaden the options for national survival.

The military problem is clear enough. It strikes at the heart of the Atlanticist assumption, so prominent in the

NATO ideal, that a seamless identity joins the United States and Western Europe.

While these military differences may be hopeless in theory, they are probably not very serious in practice. As Chapter IX will suggest, it is even possible that some American strategic thinking may, for its own purposes, come around to favoring a European deterrent. In any event, military aggression in Europe runs so desperate a risk of war that few believe any direct invasion will occur.

The real threat to European order lies in the mounting impatience with the divided and dominated Europe left over from World War II. Détente seemed to open the possibility of peaceful evolution toward a new settlement. The Harmel Exercise hoped to promote NATO as the instrument for coordinating western diplomatic policy.

As détente obviously means different things to different people, there is no immediately apparent consensus on how to go about "managing" it. It is unlikely, for example, that the French ever would have agreed to channel their initiatives to Russia through the NATO Council, any more, indeed, than would have the Americans.

The same holds true with the Germans and their relations with the Soviets: The prospects of another Rapallo, a Russo-German deal whereby Germany exchanges reunification for neutrality, must inevitably remain one of the theoretical grand options for a German settlement.*

---

* A second Rapallo might easily have more significance than the original, which was concluded when both Russia and Germany were weak and disgraced. As A. J. P. Taylor wrote: "In fact, the Treaty of Rapallo was a modest, negative affair. . . . Neither was in a position to challenge the peace-settlement; both asked no more than to be left alone. . . . There was no sincerity in German-Soviet friendship; and both sides knew it. . . . Rapallo gave a warning that

It is, after all, only a German national version of what the Gaullists have been suggesting for all Western Europe together. To get anywhere with the Russians, the Germans must doubtless dangle all the possibilities.

More political discussions of these matters in NATO might be useful, if only to make the Council's meetings more interesting, and perhaps to make particular national initiatives less competitive. But honest consultation can exacerbate as well as soothe conflicts. The interests involved in détente are too deep and the problems too delicate. Clumsy enthusiasm for détente management through NATO might well undermine whatever consensus still does exist among the partners. There is, after all, a rather fundamental anomaly in proposing to use the machinery of the bloc in order to negotiate its own demise. Given America's natural inclination toward duopoly, there is something disingenuous in our eagerness to coordinate everyone else's eastern policy through NATO.

Western diplomatic coordination of this sort has actually seldom occurred, least of all through the NATO Council. To be sure, the partners still meet periodically in NATO and solemnly intone the advantages of close solidarity and the dangers of Soviet hordes. Meanwhile, however, France, Germany, and several others all pursue their own extremely active diplomatic campaigns in the East. Periodic NATO conferences are rather like friends meeting sheepishly in church after seeing each other in more compromising circumstances the night before.

---

it was easy for Russia and Germany to be friendly on negative terms, whereas the Allies would have to pay a high price for the friendship of either." A. J. P. Taylor, *The Origins of the Second World War* (London, 1961), p. 49.

As a result of this stubborn clinging to the NATO cult, western diplomacy suffers from an increasingly acute schizophrenia. There is no real diplomatic and not much genuine military coordination through NATO, yet the appearance of an Atlantic military bloc is maintained. This is a development which is not at all in the interest of the United States, for it serves chiefly to perpetuate the view that we, rather than the Europeans themselves, can and will remain the primary guarantors of European security. This expectation is likely to be illusory—both because we will find it increasingly burdensome to continue our present military role, and because fewer and fewer Americans are likely to want to. On the other hand, as long as the NATO myth is promoted by us, Western Europeans, confident that their over-all military situation is stabilized by outsiders, are encouraged to pursue private national arrangements in the East and actually discouraged from cultivating and organizing solidarity among themselves. Hence the unsettling consequences of diminishing American engagement will be greatly exacerbated by our refusal to admit or discuss it. Europeans will not be prompted to rise to the occasion until very late and our predictions of catastrophe at our departure may thus be made self-fulfilling.

Unfortunately, NATO's decline and the dangers of not preparing for it have been obscured in the late 1960s by a precarious and misleading revival of Atlanticism. Whereas by early 1968, the process of disintegration in both blocs had accelerated to the point where it began to seem as if the European status quo was finally coming unstuck and NATO's days were numbered, by the middle of the year and thereafter, numerous developments appeared to reaffirm the status quo in general and the need for NATO in particular.

Russia's Czech intervention chilled the partisans of

Germany's *Ostpolitik*, discouraged complacent assumptions about the Soviet governing elite,[5] and aroused old fears about hordes from the East. Blocs and alliances came back in fashion and Europeans began to remind themselves of the advantages of the American presence, which had become less unpopular with the opening of the Vietnamese peace negotiations. After skirting disaster at the turn of the year, America's international monetary position improved markedly, while the Federal Republic's huge exchange surplus and reluctance to revalue relaxed hitherto stiffening German resistance to offset payments for American NATO troops.[6] Finally, de Gaulle's domestic troubles and subsequent departure appeared to weaken the revisionist forces.

All these events together conspired to give NATO a new lease on life. But whatever their long-range consequences, the Atlantic revival is more likely to prove an Indian Summer than a new Spring. For, to return to the original point, the long-run evolution of European and Atlantic affairs appears to undermine support for the kind of tight Atlantic bloc institutionalized in NATO.

Czechoslovakia did not renew the Cold War. While their reaction to the Czech crisis suggests that some people in the West would almost seem to welcome another harsh era of confrontation, they are not likely to have their wish. Today's Russians are far too conciliatory. In spite of the Czech intervention, itself undertaken with considerable hesitation and restraint, Russia obviously desired a continuing European détente and had no wish to provoke a new Cold War. Perhaps the uneasy and ill-tempered relations with China encouraged a quick Soviet restoration of an amiable western façade. In any event, in the months after the intervention, there followed not only the long-awaited strategic arms limitation talks (SALT) with the Americans, but also a veritable offensive of overtures for talks on German and general European questions. With a new government in Bonn dedicated firmly to progress in the East, the revisionist prospects in Europe quickly revived. In short, while few may have anticipated any miracles, the European atmosphere in 1970 was far from that return to the Cold War which many half-expected after the Czech intervention.

But this reviving mood of détente, while it continued to undermine the foundations of tight Atlanticism, paradoxically seemed to reinforce NATO. Many European revisionists, especially Germans, were happy enough to see America's NATO protectorate continue, as long as it proved no serious obstacle to their private diplomatic initiatives toward the East.[7] Many Germans were not eager to see their country's energies deflected into forming that close military union of Western Europe, with all its entanglements and complications for *Ostpolitik*, which a diminishing American military presence would strongly suggest.

Indeed, under the cover of loyal Atlanticism, some socialists began to dream once again of unification through neutralism, this time under a joint military guarantee by the superpowers. Revisionism and neutralism thus hoped to make their way under the cover of condominium. But whatever the prospects for that formula with the Russians, or among the Germans themselves, Germany's Atlanticist neutralism does not answer America's interest, as Chapter VIII argues in detail. For the formula sees at the end not an Atlantic Germany, but a neutral and disarmed Germany under American protection, which would increase Europe's dependence and America's burdens, and at the very time that the United States is less and less willing or able to continue its hegemonic role.

The status quo is threatened by yet another major development, the evolution of the international monetary system. Needless to say, the world's monetary system is extremely complex, encompassing as it does the broad range of financial and trade relations among most of the developed countries. While disagreement and uncertainty are widespread among economists and financiers, certain movements in the Atlantic monetary situation seem relatively clear and their likely political consequences, while beyond certainty, are not beyond reasonable prediction. Arguing these matters adequately, however, will require an extended separate study and only a few major points can be touched on here.

America's monetary hegemony forms an interesting parallel with our military hegemony. Both have grown up in this postwar period of American strength and European weakness. Both are somewhat interdependent. If, for example, the Europeans organized themselves to change the transatlantic relationship in one sphere, the political momentum might carry over into the other. Or if the United States could no longer run regular balance-of-payments deficits, it might well have to cut back overseas military expenditures.

Every imperial system needs a financial system to sustain it. The two systems go together, and if one slips the other often falls. Throughout history, empires have often financed themselves by various direct or indirect levies, at home and abroad, which, one way or another, have created the necessary resources for the system's administrative and military machinery.

The American method is perhaps characteristic of our society. We have financed our postwar system essentially on credit. As our foreign disbursements exceeded our earnings, we have simply continued to run deficits on our balance of payments, for almost every year since 1958. Because of this steady outflow of dollars, not only have our own gold reserves shrunk, from $22.8 billion in 1950 to $11.2 billion in 1970, but many countries now hold a large proportion of their reserves in dollars.[8] In consequence, the governments of these countries feel constrained to go on supporting the dollar, freely accepting it in spite of our continuing deficits, rather than risk the losses which a falling dollar would cause to their reserve savings. We have "hooked" the world on dollars.*

Many economists applaud at least the monetary side of this evolution and see no reason for change except to eliminate those still uncontrollable anomalies, like tying the dollar to gold, which occasionally allow speculators to threaten the dollar's position. Despite its academic apologists, the sustained American payments deficit has been a great source of uneasiness and a principal cause of the malaise in monetary relations which has been endemic in recent years.

In late 1967 and early 1968, the dollar's weakness produced a major crisis. Indeed by early 1968, as a result of the rapid fall in our gold reserves, many observers expected the Treasury would cease paying out gold and instead allow the dollar to "float" without its gold backing in an open currency market. The dollar was saved from this perilous if interesting expedient by the invention of the "two-tier" gold market in March 1968, followed by a temporary improvement in our balance of payments which stopped the drain on our reserves.† The

---

* Holding dollars in place of gold seemed natural enough in the immediate postwar era. In 1945 the United States had the great bulk of western gold reserves, some $20.1 billion out of $33.3 billion, and Europe's then insatiable demand for U.S. imports ensured a tolerable balance in spite of our enormous outlays.

† The two-tier gold system established two independent markets for gold—an "official" market for transactions among governments at $35 per ounce, and a "free" market, where prices have ranged

improvement came, however, not from a better American trade balance nor from a sharp drop in our nontrade outflow, but from a massive influx of short-term capital, drawn by the dollar's new high interest rates, and frightened by Western Europe's outbreak of social and monetary problems. Continuing success in balancing our payments depended upon a continuous flow of European capital to America. When Europe returned to equilibrium, the American deficit appeared again, amounting in 1969 to $7.1 billion.[9] In short, like NATO, the dollar enjoyed a false revival.

What is the likely effect of the dollar's apparent return to chronic deficit? There is sharp disagreement. One school holds that such large deficits cannot continue, that the United States will be forced to cut back its outflow abroad. A second school believes that the dollar can go on running large deficits in the future just as it has in the past. This is not only what many economists predict, but also what they prescribe. In their view, the deficits harm no one, are highly beneficial to many countries, and, by creating additional liquidity, perform an indispensable service to the international system as a whole.[10]

This last point, the need for liquidity, has become thoroughly familiar and widely accepted even by many who deplore the present system.* It is widely accepted

from a high of $43.80 on March 10, 1969, to just below $34.95 on January 8, 1970. The system, to the disappointment of private holders, has apparently succeeded in curbing speculative pressure. See John Bracken, "Gold Speculators Disillusioned," *The Washington Post,* February 22, 1970.

* Most international monetary experts agree that the world's reserves should increase in some proportion to the growing level of international trade and the secular inflationary trend of world prices. The appropriate source for this increase—gold, dollars, or some form of international specie—is a subject of constant debate. The present system's heavy dependence on dollars for increased liquidity, often called the "Triffin Paradox," is one of its key prob-

that the United States has acted since World War II as a kind of world central bank, creating by its deficits the additional credit necessary to service an expanding world economy. The United States has, in effect, assumed a financial hegemony analogous to the military hegemony exercised in NATO. The hegemonic military system is matched by a hegemonic monetary system.

The imperial character of the monetary system is even more apparent upon investigating the causes for America's balance-of-payments deficit. For although it is true that the United States had a payments deficit in every year from 1958 to 1968, during that same period we also maintained a sizable surplus in our balance of trade.

The American domestic economy sold, over-all, more goods and services abroad than it bought from producers abroad. Nevertheless, the American economy as a whole was paying out more to foreign economies than it was earning from them. Why? Compared to any other country, and in proportion to its trade, the United States has a conspicuously large outflow of funds for nontrading purposes.

In 1966, for example, the American balance on goods and services showed a surplus of $6.1 billion. The American balance of payments, measured on a liquidity basis, showed a deficit of $1.4 billion. In that same year, the government ran up $3.7 billion of military expenditures abroad and earned $829 million in foreign military sales. The net outflow for military expenditures was thus

lems, for the more the dollar is called upon to meet the demands for liquidity, the weaker it becomes, and the less confidence it inspires among international creditors. As a substitute Triffin proposed a system of international credit, created by an international authority, an idea embodied in the new IMF Special Drawing Rights. See Robert Triffin, *The World Money Maze* (New Haven, Conn., 1966), pp. 346–73.

$2.9 billion. In the same year, $4.3 billion of private capital flowed out and $2.5 billion flowed in—a net outflow of $1.8 billion. Together, the exchange losses from official military expenditures and private capital outflow totaled $4.7 billion—nearly two-thirds of the exchange deficit for that year.[11]

Insofar as these items are the determining causes of the American payments deficit, it can be said that that deficit reflects not the weakness of the American domestic economy, but the foreign preoccupations of its government and major industries. The deficit thus reflects what might be called the costs and rewards of America's empire.

In strict economic terms, no one expenditure is more "natural" than another. Americans could equally well have met the deficit by importing fewer goods and services or exporting more of what they produced. The American balance of payments in 1966 also lost roughly one billion dollars net on the tourist account. If Americans had ceased travelling abroad, we might have saved $2.7 billion in foreign exchange. But while economics may be able to eschew rating the value of one type of expenditure over another, politics cannot. For these priorities determine the character of the society itself. They are the very stuff of politics. Economics, however, does at least teach that in a world of limited abundance some choices have to be made. But to a large degree, the present international system exempts the United States from the necessity for such choices in its overseas spending. That is the significance of the persistent American payments deficit and of the system which permits it. How long can that system last?

If the tie between the dollar and gold were broken, and every central bank agreed to accept unlimited quantities of dollars, then the system would be completely self-enclosed and the dollar impregnable. We could run large deficits forever. The world's monetary system would, in itself, be little restraint on our larger political and economic ambitions. The financial system would then be as "hegemonic" as any arrangement anyone might imagine. Should particular governments become worried about being flooded with too many dollars, they could always adjust their currency's value upward against the dollar, as the Germans did in 1969.

The American government has seemed to be pursuing a policy aimed toward this goal and, at times, with considerable success. Agreements about holding dollars for gold have apparently been reached with many foreign central banks. The creation of a two-tier gold market seemingly insulated the official gold-dollar rate from private speculation and was hailed as a major step toward the ultimate demonetization of gold.

A definite victory for this hegemonic American system has seemed possible, and, despite recent setbacks, may still occur. In the long run, however, such a consolidation of America's position is unlikely. For our financial hegemony, probably much more than our military hegemony, is bound to arouse opposition from others, and will thus be maintained only with increasing effort.

The main European objections to the present monetary system, taken together, form an interesting parallel to the political arguments against America's role in NATO. The parallel should not be surprising.[12] Monetary systems, while they have their technical requirements, are to a great extent political. Europe's objections to American hegemony in the one sphere are very likely to carry over into the other.

Under the present arrangements, we are simultaneously the world's central bank and the world's principal borrower. We argue, naturally, that the money we simultaneously create and borrow is used for the general benefit. American military presence around the world keeps the peace. American investment abroad spreads our modern technology and management to other economies. In short, American hegemony is good for everyone. Nevertheless, others resent it.

They have a case. There is something to the view that we are rather like the rich man who regularly persuades his timid neighbors to loan him money, on the grounds that his spending creates a high demand for goods and services in the neighborhood, and his bankruptcy will ruin them all. A part of the loans maintains a large body of armed retainers. Most of the rest buys up mortgages on the houses of the creditors. More specifically, neither America's peacekeeping nor its foreign investment is universally popular.

Europeans are unlikely to accept the proposition that only the United States is capable of filling the role of international credit-creator. They are more likely to believe that America, taking advantage of her special position in the immediate postwar era, has unjustly preempted an international function. Even if they grant that more liquidity has been needed, and that Europe's own remarkable economic growth would not have occurred without it, they may say that liquidity can now be created in some other way—by some international body in which Europe was properly represented[13] or even by a European bloc like the Six,[14] whose collective position in foreign trade and monetary reserves at present greatly exceeds the American.* Finally, many Europeans believe

* Foreign trade, GNP, and monetary reserves, 1968, in billions of dollars.

	Exports	Imports	GNP	Reserves
U.S.	8.50	8.25	861	16.057
EEC (with outside countries)	16.06	15.50	364	25.511

Source: IMF, International Financial Statistics, 1969.

America's liquidity-creation has been excessive, or in any event, dangerously uncontrolled in its effects.*

America's deficits, after all, are the accidental by-products of the political and military objectives of the American government and the investment decisions of American business. The deficits are not the outcome of some careful calculation of the growing needs for world liquidity. Moreover, the liquidity falls like a capricious shower over the economic landscape, and where it falls may easily prove disrupting to national plans for orderly economic and social development.

To many people, growth without rational control is, at best, a mixed blessing. The ability of governments to control growth in the interest of balance and social welfare is normally regarded as one of the primary achievements of this postwar age. Limiting and directing credit and the money supply is one of the principal instruments by which governments regulate growth. Many people believe the difficulty is greatly exacerbated by the economic consequences of America's monetary hegemony, in particular in recent years by another aspect of the dollar's special role, the Eurodollar market.

The Eurodollar market is essentially the creation of private banks in Europe and rests upon the general willingness to hold dollars abroad without exchanging them. The normal banking process, starting with dollar deposits held abroad, pyramids them into a cumulative dol-

---

* The United States is often accused of exporting inflation, that is, pumping surplus dollars into European countries at a faster rate than their economies can safely handle. The result has been inflation and, by extension, the social unrest which too rapid growth brings in its train. Even those who admit the need for increased liquidity are often troubled by the haphazard nature of the present system, and the degree to which it erodes the power of governments over their own economies. See Jacques Rueff, *Balance of Payments* (New York, 1967), pp. 3–37.

lar credit several times the original. The credit pool has been estimated as high as $40 billion.[15] So long as no one who borrows in Europe changes his dollar credit into some other currency, or deposits it within the United States, the American reserve position is not directly affected at all.[16]

Eurodollar expansion reached its present epic proportions after the U.S. government put stiffer controls on direct investment by American companies. Thanks to the Eurodollar and Eurobond markets much of American private investment abroad now finances itself not by a visible outflow of dollars through the exchange market, but by a spiral of debts in Europe. American business has taken its cue from American government. Without the Eurodollar market, the pressure on American monetary reserves would probably have been much greater in recent years, or overseas American investment very much smaller.

Once again, this whole dollar apparatus raises the question of governmental control over demand within a national economy. Although central banks and various international institutions may intervene with effect in the Eurodollar market and may exercise considerable control over the behavior of their own banks, the great pool of Eurodollar credit unquestionably gives big business, especially international corporations, greater maneuverability. And it is certain that speculative flows from one currency to another are greatly swollen by the multitudinous possibilities for arranging credit through Eurodollars.[17]

It is argued that this unprecedented accumulation of capital, and hence opportunity, represents an extremely efficient use of resources, impossible in the relatively staid and scrutinized European national money markets. Without the Eurodollar, it is argued, Europe would never have developed a money market big enough to fuel its own transformation into a single continental economy. This sanguine view ignores the problems of both stability and political control.

While a whole school of distinguished academic economists and their followers may rejoice at the decline of planning, the increasingly complex and urgent social and environmental needs of modern society do not suggest that governments can or will abdicate control over the economic context of society. Quite the contrary. The cost of anarchy in the economy and the physical environment generally has seldom been more obvious or more terrifying. Chances are that governments will not stand by passively and be robbed of the powers needed for social self-preservation. In short, we are not seeing the dawn of a new era of laissez-faire.

It may well be that European national planning is obsolescent in many respects, that the high degree of interdependence demands intimate coordination which amounts, in effect, to a new form of European·political system. Granted that there is also an interdependence across the Atlantic. But the difference in the degree of economic interdependence among the Six, on the one hand, and between them and the United States, on the other, is great enough to constitute a fundamental difference in kind.* The EEC may spark a genuine politi-

---

* The relative importance of intra-Common Market trade as against Common Market trade with the United States is shown in the following figures, in millions of dollars:

	Jan.-Mar. 1968	Apr.-June 1968	July-Sept. 1968	Oct.-Dec. 1968	Jan.-Mar. 1969
Intra-Common Market exports	6798.2	6665.8	7080.9	8384.7	8506.2
Common Market exports to the U.S.	1425.3	1369.8	1468.8	1506.0	1204.8

Source: IMF, Direction of Trade, August 1969, p. 67.

cal community; the Atlantic relationship will not. The governing of Europe may increasingly center itself in Brussels; it will never willingly move to Washington. Nor will Americans be governed from Europe. Whatever the governmental arrangements may be in Europe, the control over vital sections of European economic life is unlikely to be left to an alien political system preoccupied with problems and goals of its own.

It is these larger considerations that make it a great deal less than certain that America's present hegemonic financial role will continue indefinitely, whatever the situation may appear to be in the short term. The creation of Special Drawing Rights, widely seen as an American victory, may, in fact, mark the turning point.[18] For the machinery of a real world central bank now exists, at least in embryo, and the pattern of its arrangements is not hegemonic, but more genuinely multilateral. Any cohesive EEC bloc would have a veto. The new spirit of general cooperation among the Six, and their particular emphasis upon the achievement of monetary cooperation and solidarity, suggest that such a European bloc may well begin to assert itself effectively. While no one should underestimate the great practical difficulties of organizing a coherent European monetary bloc, such a development is by no means impossible and, in the long run, seems a more realistic expression of economic and political realities.

The real problem, in financial as in military affairs, may well be how to achieve an orderly devolution without catastrophe. There are elements in the present situation which should be disquieting to even the most sanguine and phlegmatic observers. As a result of American credit-creation, officially through the balance of payments and privately through the Eurodollar market, a gigantic pyramid of short-term dollar claims has now been built up among public and private creditors, an enormous "overhang" of liquid balances which can theoretically enter the exchange market whenever holders feel the dollar's relatively stable value is threatened.[19] Again, of course, there is the optimistic view held by those who see America's present position maintaining itself and indeed gradually becoming more and more stable. If worse comes to worse, it is said, if central banks begin cashing in their dollars and U.S. gold reserves vanish, the dollar can always "float" without its gold backing on an open market where buyers and sellers would establish a going rate relative to the other currencies. In the end, such a development would not, it is said, make much difference, let alone cause a catastrophe. For their reserves foreigners will still prefer to hold dollars over gold or any other national currency. And why not? A dollar, it can be argued, is a share in the future productivity of the American economy. Given the enormous size and promise of that economy, as well as America's social and political stability, no other kind of reserve is as safe.[20]

Whatever the technical validity of this view of currency markets, the progress of inflation in America in recent years, not to mention the social and political unrest, has begun to call these cheerful assumptions into question. It seems increasingly probable that the American economy will become less competitive in international trade. Over the past fifteen years, even if our official and investment outflows have usually caused us a balance-of-payments deficit, we have always enjoyed a trade surplus. The credit we were demanding for ourselves was at least founded upon the proven ability of our massive economy to compete successfully in world commerce. But the steady decline of our export surplus into a deficit has called our competitiveness and adaptability into question. It seems possible that America's postwar commercial primacy has been based on certain advantages which time is gradually removing.

For an advanced industrial country, America's exports have always included a surprisingly high proportion of food and raw materials. The food exports are being threatened by the Common Market's agricultural policy, and, despite our protests and the winning of an occasional concession, Europeans are likely to persist in their agricultural policy. The differential between prices is likely to decline as Europe belatedly modernizes its agriculture.

Our ability to compete in industrial products, despite high wages, has always depended on an advanced degree of technology and industrial efficiency. In certain very advanced industries, like computers, we still maintain a strong lead. But in others, like nuclear power, we are perhaps falling behind.[21] Possibly even more significant is our apparently declining competitiveness in many basic manufactures—like cars, steel, and chemicals. Why? There are no simple reasons. Perhaps our advanced technology is a diminishing advantage in a world where scientific information travels with great rapidity and all countries concentrate heavily on technological education. Our own direct investment has probably encouraged the process of dissemination. Perhaps striking improvements in transport and its relatively declining cost have more and more opened the American home market to foreign penetration. In any event, the American trade balance has been falling almost steadily for the past five years.

No doubt a serious effort to check the inflation induced by Vietnam will improve the situation, but a dramatic reversal is uncertain. Perhaps instead, we are now fated to lose the overwhelming commercial pre-eminence which we gained through the ruin of our competitors in World War II. If so, the base upon which American world credit is built, while it doubtless will remain gigantic, may well be entering a secular decline.*

Other countries have gone through these periods of disequilibrium and retrenchment and still managed, by a sustained domestic deflation, to keep down their trade deficits and continue their dominating financial roles abroad. In the 1920s, for example, the British endured a million unemployed for an entire decade rather than abandon the gold standard.[22] It is questionable, however, whether the United States is in the mood for this kind of domestic self-denial. In an economy where foreign trade is no more than 5 percent of the entire GNP, protectionism or devaluation seem far more appealing routes to restoring the balance of payments than sustained deflation. An even easier remedy lies in cutting the government's expenditures abroad, particularly when the purposes of these expenditures have become unpopular with a powerful and articulate section of the country's political elite.

In summary, since World War II the United States has assumed not only the military hegemony over Western Europe embodied in NATO, but the financial hegemony embodied in our role as Atlantic central bank. Both these roles, naturally, have been closely connected and reinforcing. Our ability to create credit for ourselves by running a balance-of-payments deficit has been the means allowing us to finance the heavy exchange

---

* H. S. Houthakker, a member of the Council of Economic Advisers, argues that with an increase in national income, the U.S. propensity to import rises proportionately faster, whereas, as the national income of several major foreign trading countries rises, their propensity to import American goods shows a relative decline. This, he concludes, will cause the U.S. trade balance to worsen over time. See H. S. Houthakker and Stephen P. Magee, "Income and Price Elasticities in World Trade," *The Review of Economics and Statistics*, May 1969, pp. 111–25.

costs of our military roles in NATO and Asia.[23] The huge visible investment in Europe of so many of our large corporations has reinforced our pledges and troop commitments for Europe's military security.

In recent years, the economic as well as the military hegemony have been coming under increasing strain. Europeans appear more determined to check the unrestricted credit-creation formerly exercised by the United States through its payments deficits. Henceforth, the decisions about creating international credit are more likely to be multilateral and America's deficits more likely to meet firmer resistance. The apparent determination of the Europeans to build a monetary bloc out of the EEC, an almost inevitable concomitant to their advancing economic integration, would, if carried out, strengthen their hand in restraining the United States. The American margin for maneuver may also be reduced by a secular decline in our balance of trade. Though an end to the Vietnam War will help reduce our official foreign expenditures, our foreign exchange deficits antedate the war by several years. If the level of official and investment outflow goes on even as before the war, with a declining trade surplus, we cannot help but run ever-increasing deficits. In the face of effective resistance to those deficits, we will have to begin to impose priorities upon our national expenditures abroad, as well as at home.

The development of European monetary cohesiveness is likely to result in a more restrained and selective credit-creation in the European money market. It also seems likely that the Six will exercise more effective control over international corporations.[24] Financing American foreign investment from Europe may well grow more difficult. Competition between government and business for America's own exchange resources may thus grow sharper and, in turn, increase the pressure for military withdrawal.

Balance-of-payments problems are real enough in themselves; for many Americans they symbolize something more: the military and political overextension of the United States into the outside world. The experience of Vietnam has raised powerful resistance, both to huge military expenditures and to American commitments abroad—a disenchantment which may spread to costly and moribund alliances that seem to have outlived their usefulness. In an era of détente, the troubled state of the domestic society will increasingly seem a more appropriate target for the government's attentions. American administrations prodded by an aroused Congress may find it wise to husband their external resources for those parts of the world where they are more desperately needed. It will not be surprising if all these elements and forces gradually erode both the means which sustain our present European hegemony and even the myths and doctrines that justify it. For those who would preserve the accomplishments of American postwar diplomacy, conventional Atlanticism provides a myopic and inadequate vision for the future.

VII. THE PERSISTENCE OF ATLANTICISM

Why does Atlanticism, NATO in particular, have so tenacious a hold on the American imagination? Why have Americans, preoccupied with building a western bloc, given so little thought to the restoration of Europe as a whole? Why do the Americans prefer a Europe from Honolulu to Hamburg to a Europe from the Atlantic to the Urals?

To some extent, Atlanticism is merely the reflection of American provincial ignorance. There is little conscious knowledge in America of the great civilizations of Central and Eastern Europe or their place in European history. For many Americans, Europe's eastern half remains a barbaric hinterland where immigrants come from.

There is also de Gaulle's unkind thesis: Atlanticism, to paraphrase his comment on Roosevelt, is the American "will to power . . . cloaked in idealism."[1] In some respects, de Gaulle's view is right. Atlanticism is, among other things, the ideology of American hegemony over the West, much as communism is the ideology of Russian domination over the East. The ideal of an interdependent community of states is highly serviceable for imperialist purposes, much more so than simple democracy, with its inconvenient bias toward national self-determination.

But Atlanticism, like communism, would never have so extraordinary an appeal if it were based on only cynicism and self-interest. As an ideal, Atlanticism draws its strength from the country's highest motives and aspirations. For many well-meaning Americans, being against NATO is like being against birth control. But why is there such an investment of moral fervor in a military alliance? The answer lies in some peculiar qualities of the American political imagination, qualities which, in turn, have a profound effect in shaping American foreign policy.

The foreign policy of any country is obviously the product of many factors—elements which scholars seek to define and measure in hopes of being able to gain some rational picture of how and why policies are what they are. Ideally, analysts could build a model of the official mind, a sort of computer, which, told what objective elements go in, could predict what policies would come out. Unfortunately for the more scientific aspirations of international studies, external inputs, before they emerge as policies, must first be perceived, and therefore pass through the human imagination. Thus the foreign policies of a nation are, by definition, the product of its official imagination, reacting, in turn, to the exigencies and intrusions of the outside world.

The imagination is not merely a helpless receptacle of inputs, but is, in itself, an active element in the composition of policy. Perception requires positive, creative action by the mind. The mind must paint its own picture of the world outside before it can either see that world or react to it.

Imaginations, of course, are not free spirits, even when the outside world appears to give them a wide range of choices. Every mind has its own characteristic way of looking at things—its own set of powers and its own personal and group experiences. These condition or "program" its vision and reactions, and often make both highly predictable.

What is true of the individual mind is true of the official national mind as well. Nations often have predictable group imaginations, or characteristic stereotypes, and a general way of looking at the world derived from their own special character and history as a people. Thus, international relations is not a totally capricious discipline and scientifically minded students are rescued from secret despair.

Of course, the concept of a national or official imagination is highly abstract. Nations and governments are made up of a multitude of individuals. Leading diplomats and politicians are presumably creative men of broad experience, whose imaginations might be supposed to surpass any system of collective stereotypes. Yet it will often be found that a country's leaders have not so much left the national track upon which their compatriots are traveling as run a bit farther ahead. In a democratic age, successful leadership often consists in pointing in the direction that the mass was already heading.

The concept of the Group Mind, or national imagination, is relevant not only because ours is a democratic age in which public opinion has a great influence on foreign policy, but above all because ours is a bureaucratic age in which the real formulators of policy live in a world of their own. Policies today are often not so much the expression of individual leaders as collective products manufactured by the machinery of government. That bureaucratic machine not only greatly influences the way policy is carried out, but also, as the immediate environment within which policy makers live and perceive, greatly conditions the visions they imagine and hence the policies they formulate.

These factors, ineffable as they may be, nevertheless are indispensable considerations in trying to understand NATO's hegemony, not to say tyranny, within the

American imagination. For NATO is part and parcel of the whole mythology by which the American imagination explains the postwar world. As that world appears increasingly complex and unfriendly, we cling to the familiar landmarks of a simpler, more heroic era. The Free World, ravaged by war, was in danger from Soviet totalitarianism. We went back to Europe and organized, financed, and protected a splendid recovery. American-sponsored organizations ended Europe's quarreling and pointed the way to the politics of the future. The organizations remain—NATO above all—as guards and monuments to an American job well done. De Gaulle and other misguided leaders may try to seduce Europe back to the bad old days, but the American ideal stands for the world of the future. To abandon NATO under Gaullist pressure would be an inexcusable dereliction from America's historical duty, analogous to refusing to join the League after Versailles. We and Europe paid a terrible price for that mistake and we shall not repeat it.

All this represents a view which Americans cannot but find flattering and convenient. There is much to be said for it. Nevertheless, it so caters to the bias of our national imagination that it would be miraculous if it did not lead us into serious self-deception.

Every country projects its experience from the past into the world of the future. Our experience has made the American imagination incurably federalist. Federalism is a paradoxical doctrine, urging both the linking of independent states into larger and larger units and the devolution of central authority to smaller and smaller regions. The American view focuses very heavily on the linking and very little on the devolution. Federalism in our own national experience has been closely bound up with the successful assertion of central power over recalcitrant regions. Conceived of in this way, federalism becomes easily transformed into the ideology of American hegemony.

We are accustomed to thinking of ourselves as the first of the revolutionary modern democracies and, therefore, sympathetic to revolution everywhere. But as two wars have pushed us into international primacy, we find the revolutionary ideals embodied in the *Declaration of Independence* less relevant than the nation-building experience under our federal constitution. In that experience, and especially in the liberal view of it, order and progress were nearly always tied to the successful assertion of central rather than regional authority.

On our continent we never experienced the decisive defeat of federal power, and therein lies the fundamental difference between our "state system" and Europe's. In our great Civil War, order and progress were re-established with the victory of the central power.

Europe's experience was precisely the reverse. In Europe's great continental "civil" wars, in the mid-seventeenth and early nineteenth centuries, the "federalizing" power was defeated. Civilized order returned with the establishment of an equilibrium, a balance of power designed to prevent the mounting of any similar centralizing pretensions in the future. It was de Gaulle's hope to restore the balance in his century, as Richelieu and Talleyrand did in theirs.[2]

Americans find it difficult to understand this ideal. Many of us have an unconscious tendency to equate Gaullism in our bloc with states' rights in America. Governor Wallace and General de Gaulle are much the same, except that the General, perversely, would rather be governor than president. For many Americans, de Gaulle renounced true grandeur by refusing to take the lead in building a European federation. De Gaulle, no doubt, would regard this inhibition as his major claim to being a great European statesman. De Gaulle's heroes are not Washington and Lincoln, but Richelieu and Talleyrand, which is something Americans can seldom understand.

It might be said, of course, that whereas we have built a successful continental system, Europe has failed. Conversely, it might also be argued that Europe's continental formula is rather more relevant to the possibilities for order in a world of diverse peoples, fond of their eccentricities and jealous of their liberties.

In any event, we do see things differently, even if we often use the same vocabulary. For example, Americans frequently use the term "balance of power," in a rather special way. We see it not as a shifting balance of independent units, but as a gigantic world coalition, led by us, which enjoys unquestioned superiority over some large enemy coalition. Ultimately, having cemented our alliance and developed a special relationship with our enemy, we dream of a grand settlement, in which we, from a "position of strength," come to transcend and embrace the hostile coalition whole. Thus we would complete a world system, reproducing internationally the federal order so impressively achieved in our own continental microcosm.

If some revisionist postwar historians are to be believed, militant American visions rather than aggressive Russian ambitions have held the initiative in world politics since World War II.[3] It was the Americans, they say, who created the global Cold War, Stalin's impressive claims notwithstanding. Stalin was only a frightened conservative who knew he was overextended. It was we who cajoled the Russians, trapped by their fatal ideological pretensions, into playing the role of hostile leader, opposing us in every corner of the world. The attempt has been expensive for them, at incalculable cost to their own economic and political development. And still they have been unable to hold up their end. As a result, the principal weakness in our coalition-building has been the lack of a sufficiently credible enemy. The Russians have tried, but appear to have failed. As a result, not only is the Sino-Soviet bloc falling apart, but so is the western alliance.

But even as Russia has let us down, we have searched for new enemies, new causes, and less limiting ideologies —all designed to preserve our bloc. To be fair, it is not that we want to continue the Cold War. Indeed, our design calls for an end to it, but only if the world of blocs can be preserved and extended. For in the age of nuclear weapons and international technology, such arrangements, we believe, constitute the only sane world order.

Federalism is not the only historical experience that conditions our imagination toward blocs and the balance of power. Isolationism, too, plays its part. For an old country, America has had remarkably little international experience. Throughout our history, we have never lived with neighbors who were equals, and thus have never had to accommodate ourselves to the give and take of international power politics. For a people so devoted to domestic political horse-trading, we developed a curious scorn for power politics on the international level. Protected by an ocean, we came to see diplomacy and the balance of power, not as devices by which men maintained restraint in a competitive world, but rather as wicked pastimes of elitist governments. When all countries were democratic like ourselves, we thought, diplomacy could be abolished.

Isolationist insulation also permitted the American imagination, when contemplating the arena of states, free rein for its strong streak of utopianism, a utopianism that made us want to believe that the world is naturally harmonious unless disturbed by special wicked forces. Our isolation ensured that this utopianism, even if chastened in domestic politics by hard experience, could nevertheless flourish in our view of the international system. At Versailles, when we did finally venture into the international arena, the United States half-believed itself a sort of a *deus ex machina*, engaged in an apocalyptic intervention to crush evil and make the world "safe for democracy."[4]

Isolationism and a kind of overbearing imperialism are thus reverse sides of the same utopian coinage. It almost seems as though Americans must either run the world or withdraw from it entirely. What we cannot do is live in the world like any other nation, playing normal power politics, confident of our superiority but not aspiring to omnipotence.[5] It is not surprising that we have great difficulty in formulating realistic, flexible, and measured foreign policies. Nor is it surprising, when faced with the usual squirming world of troubles, that we continue to search for a devil, whether it be communism or plain disorder, and that we assume so easily that it is we who must lead the Children of Light.

There is another quality of ours, compatible enough with inexperience and utopianism, but surprising none the less in a people so proud of their pragmatism: we are terribly prone to abstractions. Our abstractionism takes an odd form. We are the world's political mechanics. We are far more interested in the machinery of government than in the issues and aspirations that the machinery is meant to resolve. Hence, in dealing with international affairs, the American political imagination has a strong tendency to focus on organization and to ignore politics. Our ideal, federalism, is essentially only a more advanced model of governmental machinery. Federalist progress apparently means creating larger and larger administrative units linked by common institutions. The question of a democratic political consensus to support these units seldom arises.

There is, for example, that peculiarly vacant ideal of a "world rule of law," which so swells the hearts of good people in America. No doubt this ideal, so convenient to bloc thinking, reflects something of the central role of law in American life and of lawyers in the American government. Lawyers have their own special way of looking at things. They believe they can seize and hold a volatile world within a network of agreements. When the lawyer looks at the shifting flux of world politics, his natural instinct is to write contracts to make it orderly and predictable. Thus American secretaries of state, nearly all lawyers, have covered the world with pacts.

Diplomats and historians like George Kennan, who see the world as the will and aspiration of peoples, frequently decry the tendency to cover up the realities of power with pretentious and arid legal verbiage.[6] Inside America, of course, the verbiage means something. It is related to power, indeed defines it. The lawyer can always go to court and get his contract enforced. And perhaps even more important, the dissatisfied clients can always go to Congress to get the law changed. In the diplomatic world, alas, such civilized practices do not yet prevail. We have not yet reached the "world rule of law."

The lawyer is perhaps aware that the domestic situation which corresponds to his intellectual universe is the result of a long and involved historical development. He may know how long it has taken to produce a political community where men obey the courts, where they hire lawyers rather than thugs, where even those dissatisfied with the status quo channel their conflicts through nonviolent institutions and where men agree, under certain circumstances, to subsume their private interests to the general good.

Nevertheless, when lawyers look at history, they naturally tend to focus on the growth of the law itself, on the words that reflect and register the growth of a political community, rather than on the actual political forces that create it. And Anglo-Saxon lawyers in particular see the growth of law as a process of accretion, as the product of good procedures rather than good ideas, of habit rather than will. Hence, they argue, if the world can gradually get used to legal procedures, if nations can be caught up increasingly in a network of contracts, then conflict can be elevated from force to words—taken away from the soldiers and turned over to the lawyers.

Thus apologists for American interventionism have attempted to elevate the Truman Doctrine into the beginning of a world common law. If American power can be used to uphold successfully the principle that boundaries cannot be changed by force, if we can enlist the general support of nations for this common principle, then, it is said, we will have the beginnings of a world legal system. The world, in which interdependence and international communication increase every day, has now reached a situation analogous to the early stages of modern nation-states. The United States is to play the catalytic role of the king, supported by all the forces of order and good, upholding contracts against obstreperous barons. With steadily reinforced habits of compliance, and a gradually elaborated body of agreements, there will grow up a genuine international community.

The process, admittedly, will take a good deal of time, and cannot be achieved universally at one blow, as some people naïvely hoped possible through the United Nations. Progress toward a world legal order must proceed piecemeal. Advance will be most rapid in the modern western states, with common legal traditions and close relations with the United States. And thus we return to the great importance of the Atlantic community generally and NATO in particular.[7]

All this sounds plausible and attractive. It is certainly high-minded. In fact, however, it cannot help but be seen as an excellent illustration of the usual American amalgam of utopianism and imperialism. The blueprint either assumes a general satisfaction with the status quo—a fundamental harmony of perceived interests and identities among the states of the western bloc, sufficient for them to consent to live together in a common system of law and law-making—or, more realistically, it assumes that they will cede to the United States the role of arbiter and policeman. Without such consensus or voluntary abdication, the rule of law, if it exists, will only be a mask for the rule of force.

A rule of law, after all, may just as easily be tyrannical as democratic. There are laws in prisons. Indeed, law in itself tends to be conservative. Those particularly enamored of the virtues of law and order seldom include those bitterly dissatisfied with the existing social and political system. Those who dislike the status quo generally have a more qualified enthusiasm for the advantages of legality.

In short, it is natural for other people to regard our enthusiasm for world law as a self-serving ideology, designed to preserve the enormous international economic and political advantages which fell to us from the ruin of so many others in the aftermath of World War II. Naturally Americans favor law and order in the world; we have much more to lose than anyone else.

Granted there are benefits to law and order regardless of how unjust or unpopular the laws may be. Doubtless some people must always be dissatisfied and society cannot dissolve itself to accommodate them. In any stable society, those who dislike the status quo must be persuaded to obey the law. In some societies, to be sure, persuasion rests almost exclusively on fear, habit, or trickery. But in such societies, law is bought at the cost of freedom. That is a price for law which most Americans, lawyers included, have traditionally been unwilling to pay.

In a free society, on the other hand, the dissatisfied obey not solely out of coercion, but also because there is the prospect of peaceful change through legislation. Such a legislative process requires a political system in which the people participate. It requires an organized political community which engages the loyalty of the great mass of the population.

The creation of such communities on a large and democratic scale is the principal moral achievement of modern western civilization. To live in such a free community means, in principle, living under laws and officials of one's own choosing. In practical terms, it means living within a political system which not only permits protest, but gives its members some sense of meaningful participation. To function, such a system must enjoy a sufficient general consensus so that its citizens freely obey the laws and officials, even when they disapprove of them. A free society is based, in the classic metaphor, on a tacit social contract among its various groups, a pact to live together and acknowledge a common interest and a common authority and to carry on competition within certain rules and institutions. When enough people withdraw from this pact, freedom cannot survive. That is the basic conclusion of centuries of western political speculation.

Such consensus is seldom easy to maintain. It is a melancholy fact, for example, that in several western

countries, the United States included, a visible group of
the young, who enjoy a wider sympathy, have, in effect,
withdrawn from the social contract.

So far it has only been possible to achieve democratic
political consensus on a large scale within the common
cultural community of a particular nation. Political systems based on a broader formula have had to rely on
authoritarian force to achieve cohesion, and many of
them, including the western colonial empires, have ultimately collapsed. But American enthusiasm for a world
rule of law simply ignores this vital relation of law to
the political community. Our call for a world rule of law
generally begs the basic political questions: What laws?
Who will make them? Why should they be obeyed by
those who dislike them?

Instead, Americans often unconsciously expect the
same commanding role for the American federal government internationally as it occupies domestically. This
is often what we, in fact, mean by federalism. Our imagination, with its characteristic blinders, ignores the absence of a common political will, rooted in a democratic
consensus, which makes the federal government legitimate at home but not abroad. Thus it is that many
Americans see Gaullist nationalism as just another form
of states' rights.

The reverse side of our enthusiasm for federalism is
our abhorrence of nationalism. For a generation, Americans have been taught that the world will never escape
from war until we replace the nation-state with a federal world order. America must be the federalizer.
NATO is the prototype. Thus we combine American
nationalism with world federalism. The result is that
self-righteous imperialism which we find so difficult to
renounce or even to recognize.

But the problem of world order does not yield before

these artless federalist or covert imperialist formulas. There are no simple mechanical solutions for world politics any more than there are for national politics. We cannot resolve the problems of nationalism by abolishing nations, or rather all nations except the United States. The nation-state remains very much alive, for precisely the reasons suggested above: it is impossible to organize political communities based on democratic consent within any wider context. Without that consensus, a federal state can only be imperial. Attempts to impose such an imperial order, masquerading as federalism, probably constitute a graver threat to peace in the long run than the possibility of a return to the unstructured nationalism of the prewar era.

No sane person wants to return to the degenerate state system of the 1900s or the 1930s. But to blame these particular collective failures of statesmanship and vision on the existence of independent states is rather like blaming crime on the existence of people, or disease on the presence of life. Nation-states are literally facts of life. No useful vision of a world can ignore the necessities of domestic political existence and hence the necessity of the national state. To be sure, a new international order is gradually forming itself, especially in Europe. States are learning to cooperate with each other in all sorts of novel ways. But the American federalist imagination constantly distorts our view of this evolving process. Indeed, the American penchant for viewing every instance of an intelligent organization of nationalist interdependence as another step on the road to a world hegemony—run by the United States—constitutes an increasing obstacle to the successful evolution of a stable international order.

We would do well to cease our brainless denigration of the national state as an institution. We should not take the achievements of nationalism so lightly. We are ourselves, of course, a nation-state, federal only in that we, like most modern states, delegate some subordinate powers to regional governments. The nation-state is the political formula which has allowed us to contain the searing sectional, class, and ethnic conflicts of the last century and to achieve our present measure of domestic freedom and prosperity. Such accomplishments should not be taken for granted in our own future, or indeed in the future of any major western country. For the past twenty-five years the United States has tried to be more than a nation; today we are in danger of being something less.

It is possible to believe, of course, that modern politics is on the verge of a "quantum jump" that will make the insights and formulas of the past irrelevant, that we are leaving the era of popular politics and mass social conflict, and that we will therefore no longer need the institution of the national states. Abundance and social science will solve the big political issues and eliminate the need for a strong political authority rooted in popular consent. Problems will increasingly be left to cosmopolitan experts in institutions far away from the hurly-burly of national politics or to some one country especially suited for heavy international responsibilities. It may be so. But the tumult in the international arena over the past twenty years hardly suggests that the passion and conflict have gone out of world affairs, any more than ubiquitous social unrest suggests that political leadership is becoming obsolete in domestic society.[8]

These home truths about democracy and community and law are scarcely new insights into the problems of political life. Why is it so easy for the official American imagination to ignore them? It is tempting for a professor to blame our government's ubiquitous "legal mind."

But the penchant for worthy but irrelevant visions is hardly limited to lawyers. There have been quite a few professors of international relations in government, and even they have occasionally been known to dance themselves to death before ingenious abstractions. Compared to the United States, however, few countries have given their lawyers or professors so much prominence in the diplomatic establishment.

Any understanding of the American mind in foreign policy must take account of the singular features of that American diplomatic establishment. The bureaucracy of any country forms a kind of subculture with its own form of Group Mind, whose character strongly affects not only the style and content of foreign policy, but the vision of the outside world that lies behind it. Whatever the shortcomings of the characteristic American imagination, they are magnified several times over by the foreign policy apparatus of the American government. American diplomats are not infrequently humane, skilled, worldly wise, and devoted public servants. Taken individually, they are often well aware of the crude shortcomings in America's international vision. Yet the machine within which they must operate creates a Group Mind which is a good deal less than the sum of its parts.

There are, I believe, two broad problems with America's foreign policy machine: its grotesque size, and its tendency to equate knowledge with information. The two causes, one primarily physical and the other primarily intellectual, strongly reinforce each other.

The intellectual shortcomings are especially insidious because they are so completely pervasive and unconscious. Americans are addicted to a particularly impractical form of pragmatism which assumes that all knowledge consists of facts. It therefore follows that whoever has more facts has more knowledge. As a result, an immense cargo of facts gets deposited in Washington every day. A swarming work force sets out to examine, sort, channel, and store. On the whole the result is not more knowledge, but more work. It is hard to avoid the conclusion that an occasional thoughtful embassy letter could supplant a thousand cables. Knowledge, after all, is not a dead pile of facts, but insight into the ever-changing relationships of interests, institutions, ideas, and passions. Only an active and creative mind can achieve knowledge, not a mind which is an inundated receptacle, numbed with work. Of course, as any scholar knows, fact-collecting easily becomes one of the most dangerous forms of laziness. Industry supplants thinking; the lengthy chores of accumulation replace the hard work of synthesis. Fastidious caution masks the fear of taking responsibility for judgment.

The immense apparatus of information-gathering within the diplomatic establishment not only obstructs knowledge of the world outside, but congeals thinking and communication inside. It is close to an iron law of administration that the larger and looser the bureaucracy, the more self-preoccupied and conservative it tends to be. In a small elite corps, it is at least possible for men to communicate efficiently, essentially because there are fewer of them. Ideally, they know each other and talk together, young and old, bottom and top. Other things being equal they more easily understand each other, even if they do not always agree. Subtle orders can be given and understood; complex and flexible policies can be administered with relative ease. Where there is mutual knowledge and trust, there is more likely to be a genuine delegation of authority. Where channels are direct and personal, men in the field are more likely to make their opinions felt.

In the vast heterogeneous establishment, on the other

hand, coordination itself becomes almost the principal problem. Men at the top know little about the lower levels. They have little confidence that their orders will be comprehended there, nor do they often have the time or means to check. But without confidence, there is seldom decentralization. Instead, coordination is achieved by creating a rigid Group Mind, by reducing the world to a series of stereotypes which everyone understands, linked into a loosely coherent series of doctrines which everyone learns. The bigger and more diverse the bureaucracy, the simpler the concepts must be and the more rigid the doctrines that link them. This results from the inevitable struggle of the bureaucratic organism to prevent its own disintegration.

It follows that nothing is more difficult for this vast organism than absorbing a new idea, a notion that might threaten the precarious internal cohesion. Thus the herd of stereotypes invariably tries to shoulder out the maverick. Meanwhile good people in the lower levels become progressively exasperated or apathetic over the hopelessness of communicating through the Group Mind. Thus the center, by virtue of the Group Mind, is cut off from the insights of the field. It is hardly surprising if the system of favored concepts becomes more and more remote from the world.

On the other hand, for those who stay in it, the bureaucracy becomes the real world. Indeed, the organism can often insulate itself from any irritating intrusions by undisciplined reality. Thus the State Department houses itself in a Kafka-like machine, where the sun never shines and the rain never falls, where the very air is fabricated. All the great world outside presents itself through the medium of illegible cables, expressed in the comic-book vocabulary of the collective mind. The isolation of many of the vast American diplomatic establishments abroad is hardly less complete.

Not only can a bureaucratic organism insulate itself from reality, but where it disposes of great power, it can bludgeon the world outside to fit the prevailing notions about it. Recent American experience with these tendencies has been too painful to require elaboration.

These tendencies toward abstraction and insulation do much to explain the oft-observed phenomenon of a collective intelligence greatly inferior to that of the individuals who make it up. The phenomenon, of course, is by no means limited to the United States. Thus it is, in nearly all bureaucracies, that in spite of an abundance of individual talent, outmoded policies go on, governments forever misunderstand each other, and states lumber into blind collisions which a more nimble diplomacy could easily have avoided.

Left to its own devices, the bureaucratic organism secretes itself an astrodome, and cannot escape it. Only the political king can break through the bureaucratic bubble, and not infrequently, kings go mad. All bureaucracies suffer from these diseases, but the enormous size of the American establishment, owing in part to the reigning view of knowledge, ensures that the American version of the malady will be especially acute.

Another feature of bureaucratic life distorts any imagination compelled to work within it, namely the bureaucrat's unremitting preoccupation with power. Again the peculiarities of the American system ensure that it will display an advanced case. It is not quite right to call the bureaucrat's world Machiavellian. Machiavelli had too much style, passion, and eccentricity. Modern bureaucracy is the world of Hobbes, and living in that environment inevitably affects anyone's view of the world in general.

Hobbes based his view of the political arena on the assumption that the passions of every man put him in ceaseless conflict with his neighbor. Hobbes's everyman is an isolated and lonely egotist—ever watchful, ever suspicious, ever timid, and ever acquisitive.

Hobbes may not have understood the general world of human beings, but he clearly understood the world of bureaucrats. For it is in the nature of bureaucrats that they are inevitably competitive; like all men they are concerned with their status and power—and are ever awake to preserve and extend it. In the looser world of politics, men can afford to be satisfied, indifferent, sentimental, loyal, and even generous.[9] But in the tight cage of government, these amiable indulgences are invariably costly. Whatever goes to one man must always be taken from another.

When foreign policy is left to a great bureaucracy, it invariably projects its inner world of unremitting competition onto the world outside. Inevitably it sees in every situation a contest, and unmercifully probes the soft spots of its adversaries. All the world is on the same grid of power and there are few spaces long left unfilled. The effects of such a vision on foreign policy are easily imagined. If unchecked by the political will of the country, it will inevitably overextend its government into the outside world. Where these normal bureaucratic propensities are backed by vast resources and a strong messianic impulse among the general population, there is almost no stopping it.

Bureaucracy in America has, in addition, a feature peculiar to itself—an almost feudal disorder. In the American government as a whole, there is almost no clear definition of function. Thus, the legislators direct the bureaucracy, the chief executive writes the laws, and the courts decide policy. What is true among the branches is true within the Executive as well. There is almost no job within the government which has any clearly defined functions. Every man reaches out to take what he can get.

Disorder characterizes foreign policy as much as any other field. A half-dozen major departments are nearly always involved in every issue—State, Defense, CIA, the Treasury, and often others like Agriculture, the Bureau of the Budget, Commerce, and Justice, not to mention the White House itself.

Within each department there are usually numerous subgroups and chieftains, busily allying themselves with agencies outside, eagerly struggling to grab their "piece of the action." Rival groups constantly compete to come up with the most acceptable solution to every pressing problem, and thus extend their presence and preferably their hegemony over another field of government activity. The result has been aptly described by Stanley Hoffmann as a restaurant with several cooks, each with his own stove preparing his own dish. The first man to cook a dish gets to serve the customer.[10] The product is seldom either *haute cuisine* or a balanced meal. But the president is a "crisis manager"—a busy man with time only for a sandwich. As a result, American policies are seldom the product of any profound, sustained, and well-informed reflection.

The net effect, despite the appearance of frantic change, is profound stability. Competition, under such circumstances, produces not so much new policies as new gimmicks within already accepted orthodoxies. Paradoxically it is contemplative thinking that leads to change, while busy bustle is generally the refuge of reaction.

All these broad considerations about the isolated cultural experience and the size and nature of our government do much to explain the inability of the United States to respond imaginatively to a changing world. They help to explain why, amidst general intellectual stultification and institutional pandemonium, certain monumental myths like the Atlantic community, or NATO, are so impervious to change. Once the great machine is set on its path, nothing short of a general catastrophe can deflect it. Such a government finds it difficult to sustain a flexible and measured policy or to follow any reasonable set of priorities. We are therefore too muscle-bound to play ordinary power politics. We can either run the world or withdraw from it. And what coherence there is in our policy can be imposed only by stereotypes and rigid dogmas. To stray beyond invites chaos.

In many respects, we are probably rather like our rivals the Russians. Culturally they have always been a world apart, preoccupied with their own exotic experiences, vast spaces, problems, and opportunities. For long stretches of their history, they were isolated from normal European politics. Hence they have a similar tendency to view their participation in the outside world as a special event. Their Marxist mythology has saddled them with a revolutionary utopian vision of international politics, highly adaptable to bloc-building. And even more than in America, the orthodox view of their own development ties progress to the successful assertion of central power.

The Russians too are great bureaucrats and their internecine struggles do full justice to the Hobbesian model. Since the death of Stalin, the Soviet government has seen a constant, uneasy power struggle which must make the competitive chaos of their internal machinery somewhat like our own. Perhaps that is why both countries have had such trouble in freeing their imaginations from the Cold War, and that world of blocs which is its heritage.

But is there any reasonable alternative to this world of blocs? Europeans have twice in this century brought catastrophe upon themselves. If permitted, will they not do so again? What are the prospects for stable security in a European Europe?

III. ALTERNATIVES TO NATO

The United States might one day quietly invite the Europeans to replace American leadership in NATO. We would remain in the Alliance, of course. Some of our troops might stay, if asked, but henceforth the primary initiative for organizing Europe's defense would rest with the Europeans. Our original intent, we could say, had been to shield Europe in her convalescence, which is now clearly over. We had never meant to build a permanent protectorate. To do so now would be an imperialist perversion of a sound and generous policy. We have too many problems at home for such diversions.

It is possible, if we did withdraw, that collective European defense would collapse and the separate states retreat into hopeful neutralism, scrambling over each other to reach some accommodation with the Russians. It is possible, in other words, that Europeans would prefer the potential dangers and humiliations of disunity to the responsibilities and constraints of common action. Many European governments might wish it otherwise, but there might not exist sufficient leadership, consensus, or means to maintain effective coordination.

On the other hand, the Europeans could respond by linking their forces in some form of defensive grouping, paralleling in the military sphere what the Six have evolved in the economic. The Six have managed to hold themselves in economic union because they have made up their minds that the costs of failure are worse than the trials of working together. Could that same cohesion extend itself to military collaboration?

The arrangements need not fall into the familiar patterns of NATO or the Common Market. Not every European country, for example, would need to be welded into a collective military organization. If Scandinavia were left out, its peninsula would not automatically become a communist staging area, any more than Afghanistan must now be considered a Soviet base because it does not belong to CENTO. Nor is it really necessary to have an Alliance Council where everyone votes on strategy in an elaborate multinational mock assembly.

No European power, to be sure, could play our present commanding role. But the countries with the principal military resources and responsibilities would have the principal say in working out the basic strategic questions and dispositions. And they would logically want to consult closely with the Americans. In the face of manifest collective interest, why should any of these developments be improbable?

The first question to answer: does Western Europe have the military resources to defend itself without the intimate American participation now characteristic of NATO? Any assessment involves looking at the dimensions of both conventional and nuclear defense, including in the latter the possible role of tactical nuclear weapons.

On a purely conventional level, as we have seen, official American estimates in recent years have argued that NATO has adequate forces for anything short of a massive attack on the scale of World War II.* Further-

---

* Any assessment or even comparison of conventional military strength in Europe is inevitably subject to question—partly because of unreliable and loaded statistics, but essentially because of the different forms of military organization (western divisions in Europe are often much larger than Soviet, if support troops are included, etc.), the relative state of training, equipment, and morale (e.g.,

more, the great bulk of forces in Western Europe are European. Combined British, French, and German military manpower totals nearly 1.4 million. The American contingent in Europe is only 310,000. And given the political and technical unreliability of the Eastern European troops,[1] it can be argued that the existing balance of conventional forces in Central Europe is not unfavorable to the western powers, and would remain so even if most of the American divisions were withdrawn. Without a massive troop build-up, well beyond the scale of the Czech intervention, the 300,000 Russians in Central Europe could hardly expect an easy conventional victory over a West German army of 328,000 backed up by the large military forces of Britain and France.* In other words, the present balance of European forces denies probable success to any sudden Soviet invasion. And again, any troop movements from Russia that could decisively affect this balance would take several weeks to complete and be clearly visible almost from the start. All the allies, the United States included, would have ample time to react.[2]

In short, the Western Europeans have impressive conventional armies and air forces and are not short of means for increasing the forces if they believe it neces-

---

Eastern Europe's likely contribution), or the capability of either side to mobilize and move troops to the front (readiness vs. distance, etc.). Table 1 in the appendix attempts to look at the West-East European conventional balance in broad terms. For the various arguments, see chap. II, notes 17 and 18, and chap. VIII, note 2.

* At the beginning of 1970, total British army forces in Britain and Germany totaled 151,450 troops. There were 42,300 troops stationed elsewhere (beyond Europe). In 1969 total French army forces, excluding 15,000 stationed overseas, numbered 313,000. The British kept 53,000 troops in Germany; the French 36,000.

sary to do so.* The problem lies in organizing a European command structure that would promote their effective collaboration. After long experience with NATO
and the Common Market, the task should lie well within
the technical expertise of European bureaucrats. The
particular organizational formulas typical of NATO's
interallied staffs are not necessarily the only model.
Effective military coalitions existed before NATO. Even
friendly critics find the NATO staffs excessive.[3]

But conventional defense, however well-organized,
would be inadequate without a reliable nuclear backstop.
A power which has nuclear weapons may be expected to
have the upper hand over those that do not. A primarily
self-sustaining European defense system must have nuclear weapons of its own. The real replacement for
American soldiers and generals in Europe is a European
nuclear force.

Is such a European force a practical possibility? Separate European nuclear forces already exist. No technological or military reason prevents the Europeans, in

* Comparative Military Efforts:

	Total regular armed forces (i.e. full-time) 1969	% of regular armed forces to men of military age (18–45)	Military expenditure 1968 (in U.S. $ million)	Military expenditure as % of GNP, 1968
United States	3,454,000	8.7	79,576	9.2
Soviet Union	3,300,000	7.0	39,780	9.3
United Kingdom	405,000	3.8	5,450	5.3
France	503,000	4.7	6,104	5.3
West Germany	465,000	4.0	5,108	3.9
Italy	420,000	3.6	1,940	2.7

Source: Institute for Strategic Studies, The Military Balance
1969–1970 (London, 1969), pp. 57 and 59.

some confederal combination, from mounting a deterrent likely to convince the Soviets that the risk of invading Western Europe was unacceptable, regardless of American reactions.[4] It would presumably be in our interest to see that such a European nuclear force, once established, was an effective deterrent counterbalancing the Russians in Europe. If necessary, therefore, we could provide sufficient technical aid to make the European force appear credible, and without violating the Nonproliferation Treaty.[5] Western Europeans, on the other hand, would seem to have every reason to associate their independent nuclear forces with the vastly greater American deterrent. The United States should presumably welcome arrangements to coordinate nuclear deterrents. In return, we could reaffirm our nuclear commitment to Europe and leave some forces in Germany as a token of it.

The problems of organizing the European deterrent would be thorny, but not insurmountable. Schemes for confederal nuclear arrangements are not difficult to imagine.[6] The British and French forces, even if remaining under ultimate national control, could be coordinated by a planning group within which the Germans and Italians and perhaps a Benelux representative might participate. As a possible third element a multilateral nuclear force might eventually be organized, pledged to act in certain contingencies but subject to various vetoes.

The difficulties with a confederal European deterrent are neither technological nor organizational, but political. Even if the French and the British did get together, could any conceivable arrangement satisfy the Germans as well, the most vulnerable of the Europeans to a Soviet attack? At the present time, no one wants the Germans to have nuclear weapons of their own—neither the French, the British, the Americans, the Russians, nor the Germans themselves. The German reasons are perhaps the most relevant. The Germans know that acquiring nuclear weapons would not only estrange them from their western neighbors, but also alarm the East sufficiently to foreclose, for any foreseeable future, the possibility of progress toward even a loose form of German reunification. The Germans are therefore likely to eschew nuclear weapons as long as they believe they are adequately protected by the West and have some reasonable chance for an accommodation with the East.

With the abdication of American hegemony, Britain and France, to prevent Germany from following them in nuclear weapons, would be under strong pressure to propose confederal arrangements and American connections which would satisfy Germany's reasonable fears for security.

Within a Western European coalition, the bargaining position of the Germans, even without their own nuclear force, would not be intolerably inferior. The Germans would presumably be contributing the largest land forces to the coalition. Since their financial contributions to the nuclear arrangements would be highly welcome, they could expect to bargain successfully for satisfactory participation and assurances. For it would be clear to all that without reasonable satisfaction from the allies, the Germans would inevitably be impelled toward either a separate nuclear force or a close accommodation with the Russians. For the various obvious reasons, British, French, and Germans alike, indeed the Russians themselves, should feel constrained to make the western coalition work.

The coalition's military arrangements must also take into account the thorny issue of tactical or battlefield nuclear weapons. The most direct solution would be to replace American warheads with those of a European nuclear force. But there are more interesting possibilities.

The proper use of battlefield or tactical nuclear weapons has been one of the major issues of postwar military strategy. Tactical nuclear weapons were first introduced into Western Europe as a cheap way to stop the eastern horde without having to build a comparably massive western army. But the horde now seems less formidable, and some think an adequate nonnuclear defense of Western Europe feasible with Europe's present forces. Furthermore, some American military doctrine in recent years has strongly deprecated the usefulness and emphasized the dangers of tactical nuclear weapons.[7] For a start, it is difficult to see how such weapons might be used effectively when both sides have them. Can there be any effective "firebreak" between tactical and strategic nuclear weapons? Once nuclear weapons are used in any form, mutually ruinous escalation seems dangerously probable. The only credible firebreak it is said, lies between nuclear and nonnuclear attacks.

To be sure, some believe the prospect of automatic escalation is in itself a powerful deterrent and, for that reason, favor keeping tactical nuclear weapons in Germany. But given the probability that a conventional attack would be successfully contained with conventional forces, any strategy which makes automatic escalation to mutual ruin highly probable seems unnecessarily dangerous for both the United States and Europe. In the event of a gigantic Russian mobilization or an unexpected conventional defeat, the option of using nuclear weapons would presumably still exist, even if there were no weapons actually kept with troops on the battlefield.

Under the circumstances, there is much to be said for an inspected nuclear free zone in Central Europe, including both Germanys, Poland, Czechoslovakia, and per-

haps the rest of the Balkans. Such a move might constitute the first concrete step toward an over-all European
settlement. It might be acceptable to the communists as
well, since they themselves first proposed it, in the form
of the Rapacki Plan, and have continued to do so.*

Membership in such a zone would not prevent West
Germany from joining a Western European defense system, contributing a large land army to it, and participating in its nuclear arrangements—still without possessing
a national nuclear force or having nuclear weapons on
German soil.

Like the Nonproliferation Treaty, a nuclear free zone
would also help to eliminate fears of German revenge
and thus undermine the need for Russia's military grip

---

* As early as March 1956, the Soviet Union (in the U.N. Disarmament Subcommittee) proposed an inspected nuclear free zone in
Germany. The most famous early version was the Rapacki Plan—
first introduced by the Polish foreign minister in an address to the
U.N. General Assembly on October 2, 1957. In essence, the plan
calls for an inspected nuclear free zone in Poland, Czechoslovakia,
and both parts of Germany. The various versions of the proposal
have generally included a simultaneous mutual reduction of conventional forces, and have specifically called for ground and aerial inspection within the zone. Proposals generally tend to link the nuclear
free zone to a confederal solution for Germany that would recognize
the GDR. See the Bucharest Foreign Ministers' Conference in July
1966 or the Budapest Conference of Foreign Ministers on March
17, 1969. Since January 1965, such proposals have been part of the
Soviet package advocating a European security conference aimed at
abolishing both NATO and the Warsaw Pact and replacing them
by a new "security system." Americans have criticized the conference
proposal on the grounds that the Soviets mean to exclude them.
Similarly, the Rapacki Plan was often criticized as denying ground
inspection in the communist portion of the nuclear free zone. Neither
charge has much foundation, whatever other reasons there may be
for western diffidence. For early documents, see Polish Press Agency,
The Rapacki Plan: Documents (Warsaw, 1961). For an analysis
of the more recent proposals, see Marshal D. Shulman, "Sowjetische
Vorschläge für eine europäische Sicherheitskonferenz (1966–1969),"
in *Europa Archiv*, October 10, 1969, pp. 671–84.

on Eastern Europe. But in contrast to the NPT, a nuclear free zone would also help reduce the East-West confrontation on the soil of middle Europe, to the profit of German and European reunification and the progressive evolution of communism. If the Russians have been willing to offer such an arrangement, why should the West join the communist reactionaries to defeat the reasonable forces in the Soviet world?

Our military experts used to argue that the Rapacki Plan would give the Soviets unfair advantage because, with their relative geographic proximity, the Russians could strike the nuclear free zone with medium-range missiles, while the United States would be limited to slower and more vulnerable bombers. Whatever validity this argument may once have had, it would not seem to apply in the present era of accurate intercontinental missiles and Polaris submarines. The European coalition, moreover, would presumably have weapons available in France and Britain, not to mention its own Polaris submarines.

Needless to say, the merits of a European defense coalition do not depend on the feasibility of nuclear free zones or any other such advanced hopes for a European settlement. Whatever the actual progress toward such a settlement, a viable Western European military coalition, by shifting the primary burden for Europe's defense to the major Western European states, would reduce America's external burdens without sacrificing her true interests. Prolonging the NATO protectorate, on the other hand, only serves to underwrite Russian intransigence and European irresponsibility.

Does NATO itself actually have to be done away with in order to achieve the European defense coalition described above? Could a Western European defense grouping be organized within NATO's general framework?[8] It is possible, though the effort involved might not seem worth it. Still, the preservation of a NATO façade would soothe fears in many quarters and reinforce a continuing American commitment to Europe's security, even without the present American hegemony. There could possibly be a "European Caucus" in NATO, though the problems of organizing Europe's defenses are difficult enough without insisting that they be taken within a committee of a dozen or so ambassadors. But any serious European defense coalition would have to have as its real force a directorate of Britain, France, and Germany. Italy, should she desire it, might be persuaded to occupy herself with some sort of Mediterranean "circle"—along with France and Britain.

Any consideration of means and instrumentalities for a European coalition returns eventually to the fundamental political questions: without America's heavy leadership, would Europe prefer to become a big Finland? Finland's fate is not a happy one. Why should Europeans embrace it instead of pursuing what appear to be feasible alternatives?

It is often argued that, without America's leadership, divisive interests separate Britain, France, and Germany too profoundly to permit a stable coalition among the three. Their mutual commitments would dissolve in a crisis. Russia, at some moment of intense pressure, could always persuade Britain and France not to call down disaster upon themselves to stop Russia from crushing revanchist Germany. Similarly, Russia could always play upon Germany's desire for reunification by dangling the East as the reward for neutralization—for breaking off with the western allies, who, unlike the Russians, have nothing new to offer.

Fears along these lines are understandable, but excessive. Britain, France, and Germany are serious countries whose postwar political leadership has not been notably less responsible or competent than that of the United States. Our obsession with impossible federalist goals should not lead us to overlook the tangible network of institutions and habits that now binds together the continental governments, especially those of France and Germany. Should Britain come into some close economic relationship with the Common Market, a development that seems almost inevitable in the long run, the common interdependence will be crushingly obvious. Under the circumstances, Britain and France are unlikely to be indifferent to the fate of Germany. In the extreme case, the forcible incorporation of Germany into the Soviet world would destroy forever the hopes that have sustained Europeans since the war and, in effect, take them off the stage of history. For France and Britain to look the other way while a Russian army marches to the Rhine seems a very improbable scenario.

Of course, it is always possible, in theory, that the Russians, in some apocalyptic nuclear confrontation, could stare down the Europeans. But, equally, they could also stare down the Americans, who after all have more promising prospects for a tolerable existence without Europe than do the Europeans themselves. In any event, it is hard to see how deterrence would be weakened by the addition of a European nuclear force alongside the American.

To many people, these hypothetical nuclear confrontations seem rather fanciful foundations for imagining and organizing the future. For the past twenty years nuclear powers have been extremely wary of pushing each other too far. In prenuclear days, it was not necessarily irrational, after balancing the probable costs and gains of a major conflict, to decide for all-out war. Today, nothing short of a collective death wish is liable to lead to any such conclusion. It is not easy to see what vital Russian interests would compel running the terrible risks of a massive attack on Western Europe.

German neutralism is a somewhat more credible threat to the stability of our putative Western European coalition. Neutralism was, after all, the earliest policy of the German socialists in Adenauer's time. As long as the two major parties remained polarized—one for neutralism and one for western integration—Germany's western alignment was fundamentally precarious. Since 1960, as a result of the ascendancy of Brandt and his partnership with Wehner, the socialists, while not renouncing their concern with the East, have been formally committed to maintaining the Federal Republic's western ties.*

* During the first ten years of the Federal Republic the SPD opposed Adenauer's policy of economic, political, and military integration into the western bloc as incompatible with any real progress in the reunification issue. The *Deutschlandplan* of 1959, incorporating the SPD's 1954 and 1955 proposals for a German settlement, represented the party's foreign policy until 1960; i.e., until Brandt was nominated as the candidate for chancellor. The plan's steps toward a political solution of the German problem included a zone of disengagement in Central Europe (both parts of Germany, Poland, Czechoslovakia, and Hungary), with unrestricted air and ground inspection within, arms limitations, the ultimate withdrawal of nuclear weapons, withdrawal of all foreign troops, a collective security system guaranteed by all participating powers—including the United States and the Soviet Union, and withdrawal from NATO and the Warsaw Pact. See *Deutschlandplan der SPD* (Bonn, April 1959), pp. 5–7.

Brandt had already opposed his party's neutralism. Along with his ascendancy in 1960 came a new party policy, affirming the FRG's western alliance. Defending the new policy, Brandt argued at the 1960 national conference of the SPD: "The problem is to fix the status quo militarily in order to get the necessary freedom of movement to overcome the political status quo." See Harold Kent Schellenger, Jr., *The S.P.D. in the Bonn Republic* (The Hague, 1968), p. 176.

With the formation of their Great Coalition in December 1966, both major German parties evolved a more balanced view of the relative claims of eastern and western policy, and thereby sought to resolve the dilemma of postwar German politics and to diminish the chance of future oscillations. Both parties have given up, at least temporarily, their former insistence on a single united German state, whether neutral, as the socialists suggested, or integrated into the West, as Adenauer insisted. Both parties agreed to contemplate a separate state in East Germany, within a loose confederal structure with relaxed borders. They would accept an arrangement which would reestablish a sort of unity for the ancient German nation, but stop short of reconstituting Bismarck's united German state.[9]

But the Great Coalition's "opening to the East" was balanced not only by a continuing adhesion to the American alliance, but, in addition, by a rather pointed reaffirmation of the Franco-German partnership in the West.* The French role in this German evolution should not be underestimated. Indeed, the greatest foreign support for the new German *Ostpolitik* came from Paris, where Brandt as foreign minister was often more likely to find

* Chancellor Kiesinger said in his policy declaration for the Great Coalition on December 13, 1966: "The decisive role for the future of Europe is coming to depend on the development of the German-French relationship. The European peace order desired by East and West is unthinkable without a close and trusting relationship between Germany and France. ... Together with France, America's oldest ally in Europe, we regard a solid alliance between the free, uniting nations of Europe and the United States as indispensable, no matter how the structure of this alliance will be shaped in the future in the light of the changing world. We refuse to be talked into the false and dangerous alternative of choice." This last sentence was apparently directed against former Chancellor Erhard and his Foreign Minister Schröder, both of whom believed a clear choice had to be made between close alliance with France or the United States and openly preferred the United States.

sympathy for his eastern policy than in Bonn. De Gaulle, as we have seen, not only tried to accommodate German eastern policy, but sought to assume for France a key role in promoting it. Gaullist France, constantly promoting a loosening of blocs, was to be Germany's lawyer with both the Russians and the Eastern Europeans.

Does the formation of the new Socialist-Free Democratic Coalition after the elections of 1969 suggest any shift from the foreign policy of the Great Coalition? Obviously, there will be changes. As the leading partner, the socialists will pursue eastern advances with more ardor. They may be less sensitive to pressures from Paris, friendlier to London, and less faithful to old dreams at Brussels. But they are not likely to grow so preoccupied with the East that they seriously neglect their Atlantic ties. On the contrary, the greatest danger may lie in an excessive socialist attachment to Atlanticism and a lack of genuine devotion to Europeanism. For there is a certain tendency among the socialists to seek Germany's salvation in a negotiated condominium of the superpowers, an arrangement they believe would lead a demilitarized neutral Germany to unity under a Russian-American military arch. This view, which has considerable influence in more imaginative left-wing circles, is, in effect, a refurbished version of the socialists' earlier neutralism. It is a German neutralism which accepts Atlanticism, indeed, depends on it, but rejects Adenauer's dream of a Germany firmly tied to Western Europe.

Many German socialists have always been tepid in their support of the European movement. In Adenauer's day, many used to consider Western European unity as a Catholic plot to keep Germany permanently separated from her Protestant East. Some socialists saw Gaullist eagerness for partnership in *Ostpolitik* as a French intrusion into Germany's *Mitteleuropa*. In the socialist outlook, there is, moreover, a certain aesthetic antipathy toward Gaullism and a certain broad sympathy with fellow socialists in Britain and Scandinavia. Hence there is a natural desire to ease British and Scandinavian entry into the Common Market—not least because the looser embrace of a more heterogeneous grouping would be less constraining for the Federal Republic's economic and political relations with Eastern Europe.*

German policy, dominated by such particular considerations and such a general view of Europe's future settlement, might appear in close harmony with current American policy. Germany would be a pillar of NATO, eager to get Britain into the EEC, reserved toward France, and lukewarm toward tightening Western European economic, monetary, diplomatic, or military integration. This is a set of policies which, while ostensibly obedient to American pressures, constitutes in fact a far greater threat to America than Gaullism. For it is not our interest that European stability and security should seem to depend even more on an American military guarantee, and especially not if Germany is to be demilitarized in the bargain. Whether or not we continue our present hegemonial military role in Western Europe, we have no interest in a demilitarized West Germany.

* In his speech at the EEC summit in the Hague, Brandt advocated the expansion of the Community, because—among other reasons—". . . it is in accordance with the common interests, if the Community expands at a time during which we are striving for a more intense growing-together between East and West." He also stressed the necessity for finding a way to include the nonaligned European nations and denounced the ideal of Europe as a new bloc: ". . . we are surely agreed that our Community shall not be a new *bloc*, but a model system suitable as an element in the construction of a well-balanced all-European peace system. In this spirit, the Federal Republic of Germany is seeking an understanding with the East in cooperation and coordination with her partners in the West." See *Frankfurter Allgemeine Zeitung,* December 9, 1969.

In seeing our true interest, we must not allow NATO's propaganda about western weakness, now so thoroughly discredited, to obscure the realities of the European military balance. With West Germany armed and linked either to NATO or to a Western European coalition, an effective conventional military balance exists between Europe's eastern and western halves. But without the Federal Republic no indigenous conventional balance is possible. Any arrangement which trades German conventional disarmament for a Warsaw Pact reduction in Eastern Europe is a very bad bargain for the United States.* A good case can be made that the American army is unnecessary for Europe's conventional defense, but the German army remains indispensable. Without it, the principles of flexible response are gone, and any American commitment can be maintained solely by the old threat of nuclear retaliation—not a comforting prospect when the strategic nuclear balance is moving inevitably toward Soviet-American equality.

In any event, given the real doubts which any responsible American government must have about our future ability to maintain present commitments, let alone heavily increased ones, we ought to be encouraging rather than resisting a European defense coalition to replace NATO. A Western European military grouping run by the Europeans and allied loosely with ourselves —a coalition which cemented Franco-German partnership and tied Britain firmly into Europe—would repre-

* It must be seriously questioned whether we should desire any immediate large-scale Russian military withdrawal from Eastern Europe. At their present level, Russian troops are not a military threat. Painful experience suggests that precipitate liberalization ultimately offers great support to reactionary Soviet repression, as indeed would a too rapid western economic penetration, especially German.

sent the best evolution we might expect from our present excessive role in NATO.

It would not only be the best solution for us, but surely the best solution for Europe. Nobody knows how Germany's division may ultimately be healed and a more normal European community restored. It may or may not be possible to establish some modern version of the Holy Roman Empire, a loose bond tying together the states of Germany and opening out to the non-Germans to the east and south. Such an evolution would doubtless be a great, if somewhat ironical, improvement for the Germans and their Slavic neighbors. In the long run, it would probably be better for the Soviet Union. Perhaps, therefore, Russia can be persuaded to find military security through some means more imaginative than the present heavy-handed protectorates. Hence the hopes for some form of nuclear free zone.

No one can predict the success or final form of Europe's transformation out of the Cold War. No one can say, for example, whether communist societies can find the way out of their current difficulties without some violent or destructive upheaval. No one can say whether Russia and China will compose their differences. Who can safely predict whether the East German state can ever flourish in an open Europe?

But western statesmen are obliged to seek the way back to an open and stable Europe. And while there is much that America can neither predict nor affect, we can undertake that devolution of our own exaggerated role which will encourage the creation of that solid Western European integration, without which any real stability in Europe is hardly imaginable.

Whatever mistakes we have made in Europe since World War II, we have never yet lost sight of this one home truth: Our whole policy has served to bind Germany to her western neighbors. Today, America's stubborn clinging to NATO hegemony is the principal obstacle to Western European integration and the principal incentive to German neutralism. It would be a most depressing irony if our fatuous devotion to the decaying abstractions of Atlanticism were to destroy the greatest achievement of our postwar diplomacy.

X. EUROPEAN INDEPENDENCE AND THE AMERICAN INTEREST

Devolution in Europe would constitute a major departure in American foreign policy, even if it corresponds more closely to our original intentions in the late 1940s than the institutionalized attempt at hegemony that now exists. If, in the end, we cannot bring ourselves to do it, no one should be surprised. Power is never easy to give up. Empires are seldom abdicated voluntarily. A comfortable status quo will always find convinced defenders, whose imaginations will find intolerable perils lurking beyond each small step toward change.

In recent years, as Europe has grown more assertive, it has been fashionable to point up the potential dangers to America of European independence. A new Europe, it is said, would subject us to ruthless economic and political competition, already prefigured in our quarrels with the Common Market over trade.

These arguments underestimate American strength—as greatly as the companion argument that we should maintain perpetual hegemony tends to overestimate it. No doubt an independent Europe would become more visible in other parts of the world. But American business abroad is not a tender plant, nor are American diplomats reticent about maintaining the American interest as they see it. The argument that Europeans in the Common Market are naturally protectionist in comparison with free-trade America does not stand serious and fair-minded investigation. And European generosity in giving aid considerably exceeds our own. Indeed, Europeans appear to have abandoned their colonialist perspectives toward the Third World and, in this respect, should perhaps be imitated rather than criticized by the United States.

But the real problem is a nuclear force for Europe. Without it, Europe cannot but be an American protectorate. Would a resurgent Europe, armed with nuclear weapons, be a danger to world peace? Would it confuse or destabilize the world's power structure? This question touches, in turn, not only the problems of a nuclear Europe's own likely propensities, but the larger issue of nuclear proliferation generally.

In spite of all the writing and debating on nuclear questions, the real issues are often avoided. American liberals in particular, eager to reduce American foreign commitments, have not faced the nuclear implications of their line of policy. Indeed, in and out of power, liberals have seemingly suffered from schizophrenia over the nuclear issue. They have opposed American troop commitments abroad, and, at the same time, they have opposed nuclear proliferation. On the conventional level, they want pluralism, on the nuclear, duopoly. But proliferation and disengagement are two sides of the same coin.[1]

If the United States is to continue extending nuclear guarantees to its major allies around the world, thereby discouraging them from developing credible deterrents of their own, then any real reduction of America's worldwide military commitments is improbable, and likely to be dangerous when it occurs. If a country's defense ultimately depends exclusively on us, if American cities are hostages for it, then any responsible American government must continue to maintain the major say in that country's military arrangements. To continue the commitments but to lose control over the local events is a policy which will appeal to no sane government. Furthermore, we will have every reason to keep substantial forces in guaranteed regions to convince any would-be aggressor of the seriousness of our pledge. Hence NATO and the other pacts and bilateral military arrangements that cover the world. Hence, too, the tendency of so many liberals once in power, to pursue condominium and forget about disengagement, despite their supposed aversion to imperialism.

The only real alternative to American military imperialism would seem to lie in the creation, as circumstances permit, of genuine regional balances of power, which must perforce include nuclear deterrents when any one power in the region already has them. Clearly an effective nuclear deterrent in Western Europe is essential if we are to disengage from our military hegemony there. As the Chinese develop serious nuclear capabilities, a Japanese nuclear force will be essential if we are to disengage from our military hegemony in the noncommunist rimlands of Asia.

There are evident risks in nuclear disengagement and proliferation. But as technology ensures that our homeland will be increasingly vulnerable, basing the defense of allies upon our willingness to enter into nuclear confrontation on their behalf seems a policy no less threatening to our well-being. The logical conclusion of such a policy calls for a first-strike capability against the Soviet Union. Only then could we safely guarantee the nuclear defense of our European allies.

An antiballistic missile defense, no matter how fantastic its expense, is unlikely to offer security in a direct confrontation with a major nuclear power. It might give us a few more years of invulnerability against China, but an ability to intervene with impunity on the doorstep of a great power must come to an end in Asia, as it has in

Europe. American governments now say, or at least suggest, they would sacrifice New York and Chicago for the sake of London and Paris. If there were a serious Chinese nuclear force, would we give up San Francisco and Los Angeles for Tokyo and Bangkok? Such would seem the logical conclusion of our present nuclear policy.

Whatever the validity of this general argument for a selective expansion of the nuclear club, an independent European deterrent which, after all, already exists in some degree, would constitute, in itself, an unlikely threat to world peace. Europeans, it should be noted, have almost entirely divested themselves of those military and political extensions into the Third World which now constitute such a source of friction and danger for the superpowers. Unlike Russia or the United States, the Europeans are almost purely national rather than imperial powers. They would be unlikely to use their deterrent for anything short of a massive attack on their own homelands. Of all conceivable world powers, the Europeans would be the most conservative. A major nuclear war would destroy Europe forever. These considerations would apply equally well to the Germans should they ever have a national force of their own.*

* The issue of proliferation is often confused by the assumption that there is no halfway house between condominium and an almost universal dispersion. Leonard Beaton, in a study published in 1966, distinguished between two kinds of proliferation, that of advanced industrial states capable of building "a small force of Super-Power quality" and the "guerrillas." The former, from French and British experience, would cost roughly $20 billion over twenty years. Subsequent cost would depend on the evolution of weapons technology. Such a force was within the industrial capabilities of Germany and Japan, with Canada, Sweden, and Italy not far behind. "Small and insecure" forces, would lie within the resources of a considerable and probably growing number of lesser industrial powers in Europe and the Third World. See Leonard Beaton, "Capabilities of Non-Nuclear Powers," *A World of Nuclear Powers*, ed. Alastair Buchan (Englewood Cliffs, N.J., 1966), pp. 13–38.

The potential danger to the United States of an independent Europe, although a frequent theme in recent years, has never been part of any official American view. We have never stopped supporting the ideal of a united Europe, based, to be sure, upon our own federal formula. We have continued to hope for a twin pillar, an equal partner for America within our common Atlantic community. There is something rather touchingly narcissistic in the standard American view about the significance of European unity. Europe is to be a sort of transatlantic Jane for the American Tarzan, so that together they may share the burdens of international peace keeping.

There might, however, be some advantages to a self-sustaining Europe beyond finding a symmetrical partner for the United States. The resurgence of Europe's peoples would thrust apart the superpowers from their prolonged and increasingly inane confrontation along the Iron Curtain, and might even deflate somewhat the apocalyptic pretensions that have prevailed for so long among the "duopolists." Perhaps both the superpowers might turn away from their increasingly lunatic arms race and take a less universal view of themselves and a less commanding and more generous view toward the rest of the world. Perhaps they might even come to believe that their greatest contribution to the world community lay in the civilization which they achieved at home, rather than the power they exerted abroad.

APPENDIX TABLE 1

Army Forces of Western and Eastern European Countries, 1969.

The Central Front

WESTERN EUROPEAN ARMY FORCES

	Army forces now in W. Germany	Total army forces excluding troops stationed overseas
Belgium	—	78,000[a]
Britain	53,000[c]	151,500[b] (excluding 42,300[c] overseas)
France	36,000	313,000 (excluding 15,000 overseas)
West Germany	328,000[a]	328,000[a]
Netherlands	—	82,000[a]
Total	417,000	952,500

EASTERN EUROPEAN ARMY FORCES

	Army forces now in GDR & CSSR	Reinforced army forces
Soviet Union	300,000	840,000[c]
East Germany (GDR)	90,000[a]	90,000[a]
Poland	—	185,000[a]
Czechoslovakia	175,000[a]	175,000[a]
Total	565,000	1,290,000[b]

The Southern Front

WESTERN EUROPEAN FORCES

	Total army forces
Italy	313,000
Greece	118,000
Turkey	400,000
Total	831,000

APPENDIX

EASTERN EUROPEAN FORCES

	Reinforced army forces
Soviet Union	100,000[d]
Bulgaria	125,000[a]
Hungary	90,000[a]
Rumania	170,000[a]
Total	485,000

Scandinavia

WESTERN EUROPEAN FORCES

	Total army forces
Denmark	28,000
Norway	21,000
Sweden	600,000
Total	649,000

EASTERN EUROPEAN FORCES
[See note c.]

---

[a] Total army forces.

[b] As of January 1, 1970. Derived from *Statement on the Defense Estimates 1970*, Cmnd 4290 (London, 1970).

[c] Russia has a 2 million man army of about 148 divisions. Russian divisions are roughly 10,000 men apiece; thus about a half million men remain as support troops. Of these 148 divisions, 60 are believed to be in European Russia. With support troops, such a force might total roughly 900,000 men. Theoretically this force could be sent in varying proportions to the Central or Southern Fronts, or Scandinavia. It is said in *The Military Balance, 1969–1970* (p. 7) that three-fifths of the 60 divisions are probably earmarked to reinforce the Central Front. Hence the figure above of 840,000 Russians (a reinforcement of 540,000).

Experts have many legitimate points of disagreement on these matters. Considering the military buildup on the long Chinese border, I believe these estimates are generous to the Soviets. The mobilization and shifting of all these forces, of course, would be a lengthy and visible process and would allow time for American reaction. For the buildup on the Chinese border, see ISS, *Strategic Survey* (London, 1970), pp. 66–72.

Naturally, all these figures represent only a crude estimate of relative military strength. Equipment, training, morale, leadership, distance, surprise, etc. are all elements of great significance. Nevertheless, the table suggests that the Western European states are not notably short of military manpower. For further refinements and arguments, see chapter II, notes 16, 17 and 18 and chapter VIII, note 2.

[d] For an estimate of the troops available for the Southern Front, see *The Military Balance, 1969–1970*, p. 62, and note c above.

Sources: Institute for Strategic Studies, *The Military Balance, 1969–1970* (London, 1969), and for Britain: *Statement on the Defense Estimates 1970*, Cmnd 4290 (London, 1970).

APPENDIX TABLE 2

Some Elements in the U.S. Balance of Payments
(billions of dollars)

Year	Balance on goods and services[a]	Liquidity basis[a]	Official reserve transactions basis	U.S. private capital, net flow	Foreign capital, net flow	U.S. government grants and capital, net
1965	+7.1	−1.3	−1.3	−3.8	+0.3	−3.4
1966	+5.3	−1.4	+2.6	−4.3	+2.5	−3.4
1967	+5.2	−3.5	−3.4	−5.7	+3.4	−4.2
1968	+2.5	+0.2	+1.6	−5.2	+8.6	−4.0
1969[b]	+1.9	−10.8	+1.9	−6.2	+3.0	−4.0

+ and − indicates effect on balance of payments

[a] For definition, see chap. 6, note 9.

[b] Average of the first three quarters on a seasonally adjusted annual rates basis. For revised 1969 figures, see U.S. Department of Commerce, *Survey of Current Business*, March 1970, p. 27.

Source: Economic Report of the President, February, 1970, pp. 276–77. In the full table, several qualifications are introduced in the footnotes and there is a substantial item for errors and omissions.

APPENDIX TABLE 3

Some Elements in the U.S. Monetary Position, September 1969
(billions of dollars)

Gold and monetary reserves	16.74
U.S. external claims	12.22
Short-term	8.95
Long-term	3.27
U.S. external liquid liabilities	42.65
By creditor: to central banks & gov'ts	12.48
to other banks & other foreigners	28.43
to international agencies	1.74
By type: short term	39.85
marketable	1.03
nonmarketable convertible	.75
Fund gold deposit & investment	1.02

Source: IMF, *International Financial Statistics*, Jan. 1970, p. 375.

NOTES

Chapter I

1. Alexis de Tocqueville, *Democracy in America*, trans. Henry Reeve (New York, 1959), vol. I, p. 452. For a modern rendering, see Kenneth Waltz, "Stability in a Bi-Polar World," *Daedalus*, Summer 1964.

2. See Raymond Aron, *Peace and War* (New York, 1968), p. 493.

3. Much writing exists on the subject. For a discussion of many of the points raised in my text, see Stanley Hoffmann, *Gulliver's Troubles* (New York, 1968), pp. 43–46, 133–35.

4. See former Budget Director Charles L. Schultze, testimony, U.S., Congress, Joint Economic Committee, Subcommittee on Economy in Government, *Hearings, The Military Budget and National Economic Priorities* (Washington, D.C., 1969), part I, p. 49.

5. Institute for Strategic Studies, *The Military Balance, 1969–1970* (London, 1969). Figures are for total armed forces of NATO countries worldwide. (See chap. II, note 11, below.) Manpower comparisons give a crude, if straightforward measurement of relative strength. Obviously, factors such as equipment, training, morale, leadership, and distance are highly relevant. For refinements and disagreements, as well as figures for air and naval forces, see the works mentioned in chap. II, notes 17, 18 and 19 and chap. VIII, note 2. For an extended comparison, see Table 1 in the appendix.

6. Office of the Assistant Secretary of Defense, Systems Analysis, *Evaluation of NATO and Pact Conventional Forces in Central Europe* (Washington, D.C., October 1968).

7. For figures and a breakdown of defense spending on a state-by-state basis, see Juan Camaron, "The Case for Cutting Defense Spending," *Fortune*, August 1, 1969, pp. 69–75.

8. Hannah Arendt, *Origins of Totalitarianism* (New York, 1966), pp. 125ff.

9. For a discussion, see Alastair Buchan, "The United States as a Global Power," Canadian Institute of International Affairs, *International Journal*, Spring 1969, pp. 207–28.

10. The writings of George Liska are a distinguished exception. Imperialism, he openly argues, is essential to international order. See his *War and Order: Reflections on Vietnam and History* (Bal-

timore, 1968). Former Under-Secretary of State Eugene V. Rostow, while he eschews the term imperialism, similarly emphasizes the necessary role of America's power in maintaining general order. See his *Law, Power and the Pursuit of Peace* (Lincoln, Neb., 1968).

11. "For the United States to reduce its international involvement for the sake of domestic peace and justice only to find both eluding it in a constricted and at once contentious and embattled parochial existence would be the supreme irony of American politics. A great power should not incur this risk in a vain quest for immunity from history's tragic dimension. The awe of gods and men is easier to bear than their laughter." Liska, *War and Order*, p. 115.

Chapter II

1. NATO's ambiguity was heightened by the way it was sold to the American public in four distinct stages: first, the Vandenberg Resolution of June 1948—a commitment in principle to the concept of regional groupings; second, the treaty itself, in April 1949; third, a commitment to military aid in the Mutual Defense Assistance Program, October 1949; and, finally, a commitment of American troops and leadership in June 1950. With some reason, critics complained that the Alliance in bloom did not much resemble the picture on the seed package. See chap. II, note 5, below.

Russia's atomic explosion of September 1949, and the onset of the Korean War in June 1950, greatly encouraged the transition into the two final stages. The rationale was ready for the president by April 1950 (before Korea) in "National Security Council 68," a broad strategic study which, in effect, called for the partial mobilization that has characterized the United States ever since. For discussions of this period, see Dean Acheson, *Present at the Creation* (New York, 1969), pp. 374ff; Coral Bell, *Negotiation from Strength* (New York, 1963), pp. 3–67; Seyom Brown, *The Faces of Power* (New York, 1968), pp. 31–62; W. McGeorge Bundy, *The Pattern of Responsibility* (Boston, 1952); and Hearings before the Personnel Security Board, *In the Matter of J. Robert Oppenheimer* (Washington, 1954).

2. Dean Acheson, radio address, March 18, 1949. *Department of State Bulletin*, vol XX, pp. 384–88.

3. Kennan, one of the few with any deep knowledge of the Soviets, had expected a reaction to the Truman Doctrine and the Marshall Plan, and was not surprised in 1948 by the Czech coup or the Berlin blockade. While among the first to deflate utopian expectations of intimate Soviet-American cooperation, he saw the Soviet European policy dictated by defensive Russian national interests and not

ideological designs for continental domination. George F. Kennan, *Memoirs* (Boston, 1967), chap. 15.

4. Kennan favored an American-Canadian nonreciprocal guarantee to the Brussels Pact. *Memoirs*, pp. 406–9.

5. U.S., Congress, Senate, Foreign Relations Committee, *Hearings on the North Atlantic Treaty* (Washington, D.C., 1949), part I, p. 47. By this reply, Acheson notes in his *Memoirs*, he meant that Article 3 of the treaty would not oblige us to keep an army in Europe. He also notes that his testimony was given "a year before the [transatlantic] United Command was thought of." According to McGeorge Bundy, Acheson, shaken by the unexpectedly early Russian nuclear test in August or September of 1949, became a principal leader urging American and Allied rearmament. Korea provided the decisive event, winning the government to Acheson's policy. Bundy, *The Pattern of Responsibility*, p. 77.

6. See especially, "Agreement Between the Parties to the North Atlantic Treaty Regarding the Status of their Forces" (London, June 19, 1951); and "Agreement on the Status of the North Atlantic Treaty Organization, National Representatives and International Staff" (Ottawa, September 20, 1951). NATO Information Service, *NATO, Facts and Figures* (Brussels, 1969).

7. The American commitment to Europe did not originally make out cities nuclear "hostages." Only after Sputnik in 1957 were they seen to have acquired this status. In any event, according to John J. McCloy, our original commitment presupposed no imminent Russian attack, but sought to correct a military imbalance in Europe and thus provide a sense of security to permit economic and political renewal. McCloy, *The Atlantic Alliance: its Origin and its Future* (New York, 1969).

8. General André Beaufre, *NATO and Europe* (New York, 1966), pp. 34 and 41.

9. See Alastair Buchan, "The Future of NATO," *International Conciliation*, 1967, pp. 19–20.

10. Before French withdrawal, Beaufre had forcefully expressed French indignation: ". . . in the whole of this complex, overstaffed organization the United States holds the most important commands (seven out of thirteen), Great Britain has five subordinate commands, and France has *only one* subordinate command. . . . It would be difficult to claim that the present division is an entirely fair one; and it should be noted here that French requests have never been taken into consideration." Beaufre, *NATO and Europe*, pp. 37–38.

11. Manpower comparisons of Warsaw Pact versus NATO forces, i.e., forces "assigned" to NATO, give a somewhat misleading picture of Western European military forces in being. Of the three principal Western European military powers, only Germany,

with an army of 328,000, assigns the great bulk of it to NATO. In early 1970, of Britain's 193,000-man army, roughly 56,000 were in the BAOR (Rhine army) assigned to NATO, although, according to Defense Secretary Healey, 70,000 more could reinforce, and an additional 20,000 from the Strategic Reserve were earmarked for NATO. France assigned none of her 328,000-man army, although about 36,000 were stationed in West Germany under a bilateral agreement. Institute for Strategic Studies, *The Military Balance, 1969–1970*; Denis Healey, "NATO, Britain, and Soviet Military Policy," *Orbis*, Spring 1969; *Statement on Defense Estimates 1970*, Cmnd 4290 (London, 1970).

12. The actual procedure for calling up forces in the event of an emergency is not part of the public domain, but in any case would vary according to the nature of the crisis. While the command staffs have endeavored to draw up contingency plans anticipating every eventuality, no country is actually committed to following them. In an emergency, SACEUR may command, but there is no guarantee that the member countries will follow.

The procedure for the use of nuclear weapons is, if anything, more uncertain. A request from the field to use nuclear weapons would be passed to SACEUR who in turn would pass it to the NATO Council. Upon unanimous agreement in the Council, the request would then pass to the president of the United States, who would decide. The effectiveness of such procedures in a dire emergency has been questioned. See Drew Middleton, *New York Times*, March 21, 1969. Reports of the December 1969 Ministerial Conference implied a streamlining, although against German protests. See *New York Times*, December 4, 1969.

13. In August 1964, planes from the Turkish air force, all assigned to NATO, conducted a bombing mission on Cyprus. See T. W. Adams and A. J. Cottrell, *Cyprus Between East and West* (Baltimore, 1968), pp. 63–67.

14. The NATO organization is served by at least 33 categories of committees. See Bjarne Erikson, *The Committee System of the NATO Council* (Norway, 1967), pp. 34–35.

15. The amount given in a statement by Under-Secretary of State Katzenbach, press conference, January 9, 1968, *Department of State Bulletin*, January 29, 1968, p. 142. See also chap. VII, note 24, below.

16. For a discussion of shifting strategies and force levels, see A. J. Cottrell and J. E. Dougherty, *The Atlantic Alliance: A Short Political Guide* (London, 1964). By 1968, U.S. forces in EUCOM were down from 417,000 in 1961, to 316,000. Senator John Sherman Cooper, "Report to the Military Committee of the North Atlantic Assembly," Fall 1969. (*Mimeo.*)

17. Statement by Secretary of Defense Robert S. McNamara, *The Fiscal Year 1969–73 Defense Program and the 1969 Defense Budget* (Washington, D.C., 1968), pp. 27–32 and 80–82.

18. Office of the Assistant Secretary of Defense, *Evaluation of NATO*, signed by then Assistant Secretary of Defense Alain Enthoven. Air and naval forces are also included. See also the statement of British Defense Secretary Denis Healey, British Information Service, *Defense: Perspective of Soviet Military Policy,* February 5, 1969.

19. A recent statement of this cheerful view is found in Alain Enthoven and K. Wayne Smith, "What Forces for NATO and From Whom," *Foreign Affairs*, October 1969, pp. 80–96. Air and naval forces are included. This "systems analysis" approach to strategic thinking relies heavily upon favorable judgments of western equipment and training. For a hostile critique, see U.S., Congress, House, Special Subcommittee on National Defense Posture of the Committee on Armed Services, *Review of a Systems Analysis Evaluation of NATO vs. Warsaw Pact Conventional Forces* (Washington, D.C., September 1968).

20. Institute for Strategic Studies, *The Military Balance, 1969–1970*. These manpower figures give an admittedly crude, if straightforward comparison. For refinements and disagreements, as well as figures on air and naval forces, see the works in notes 17 and 18, above, and chap. VIII, note 2. Figures cited in the text are for total Western European military forces, not just those "assigned" to NATO. For an extended comparison of army forces, see Table 1 in the appendix.

21. *Ibid.*

22. The immediate effect of losing the French forces actually assigned to NATO was serious if not catastrophic. The 36,000 French troops in Germany remain under a bilateral agreement. France participates in the new NATO Defense Ground Environment System (NADGE) but her air force, some 450 planes, has been withdrawn from the automatic air defense system.

23. The United States was also forced to give up its numerous bilateral supply and air facilities developed for NATO support, valued at some $846 million. U.S., Congress, House, Armed Services Committee, *Report of the Special Subcommittee Visiting American Military Installations and NATO Bases in France* (Washington, D.C., September 1966), p. 10379.

24. Air rights have been renewed yearly, but if unavailable in a crisis, the central and southern fronts would be separated and the maneuverability of NATO aircraft and airborne forces seriously constricted. If land supply across France, now denied, remained closed during a conventional attack on Germany, American forces in

Bavaria would have to be supplied entirely through the crowded Low Countries and down the Rhine. As there would be no direct connection between Italy and the north, NATO would be cut in two.

Chapter III

1. Louis J. Halle, *The Cold War as History* (New York, 1967), p. 86.
2. Nowhere, as Halle notes, was the "brooding terror" of the Cold War more accurately captured than in J. R. R. Tolkien's magnificent trilogy, *The Lord of the Rings* (Boston, 1954–56), 3 vols.
3. For the roots of the Open Door policy, as well as its extension to Europe, see the learned and provocative William A. Williams, *The Tragedy of American Diplomacy* (New York, 1961). For a voluminous and highly critical account of America's wartime diplomacy, see Gabriel Kolko, *The Politics of War* (New York, 1968).
4. For Stalin's restraint on the Yugoslavs over Greece, see Milovan Djilas, *Conversations with Stalin* (New York, 1962), p. 164. See Halle, *The Cold War as History*, chap. 9.
5. See Gar Alperovitz, *Atomic Diplomacy* (New York, 1965), a fascinating if selective interpretation.
6. Adam Ulam, *Expansion and Coexistence* (New York, 1968), p. 356.
7. *Ibid.*, p. 355.
8. See Kolko, *The Politics of War*, pp. 31–63 and 172–93.
9. The varying accounts of the Polish question at the Teheran Conference make fascinating reading. See Ulam, *Expansion and Coexistence*, pp. 351ff and Kolko, *The Politics of War*, chaps. 5–7. For what Ulam describes as Churchill's "shamefaced account of the exchange" (p. 353), see Winston Churchill, *Closing of the Ring* (Boston, 1951), pp. 361–62 and 394–97. Churchill's account clearly suggests agreement among the Three about moving both Russia and Poland westward at Germany's expense, even though all had misgivings about getting the London Poles to agree.

No one appears to have made a firm declaration of support for the London Poles. Churchill, as Ulam notes, apparently did not even defend them against Stalin's charge of collaboration (Ulam, p. 354). Russia, which had already broken off diplomatic relations with the exile government, was willing, Stalin said, to renew relations, but was doubtful that the Polish government (London) "would ever be the kind of government it ought to be" (Churchill, p. 395). Churchill, noting that the new Poland "had been given a fine place to live in" agreed to seek the exile government's approval. The passage continues: "Stalin said that it would be a large, industrial State, 'And friendly to Russia,' I [Churchill] interjected. Stalin replied that Russia wanted a friendly Poland" (Churchill, pp. 396–97).

10. Ulam, *Expansion and Coexistence*, p. 400.

11. For example, *ibid.*, p. 405; and Halle, *The Cold War as History*, pp. 185–86. Khrushchev's figures were listed publicly in *Pravda*, January 15, 1960. Russians consistently use these figures. Some western scholars are more skeptical than Ulam. For a lengthy discussion, and a more cautious view, see Thomas W. Wolfe, *Soviet Power and Europe, 1945–1969* (Baltimore, 1970), pp. 16ff and notes.

12. Halle argues that Russia, frustrated by western successes in Europe, turned to Korea which, lacking an explicit western military guarantee, would be hers for the taking. Halle, *The Cold War as History*, p. 204. Others argue that Korea was primarily a tactical diversion to involve the United States in an Asian war and create new opportunities for the real prize, which was Europe. Brown, *The Faces of Power*, pp. 53–62. For further discussion, see chap. IV, note 1 and chap. II, note 1.

13. Ulam, *Expansion and Coexistence*, pp. 414–15.

14. For widely differing accounts of Roosevelt's postwar vision, see Willard Range, *Franklin D. Roosevelt's World Order* (Athens, Ga., 1959); and Williams, *The Tragedy of American Diplomacy*. For de Gaulle's attitude toward the Roosevelt vision, see pp. 58–59, above.

15. "... nowhere in Washington had the hopes entertained for postwar collaboration with Russia been more elaborate, more naïve, or more tenaciously (one might almost say ferociously) pursued than in the Treasury Department." Kennan, *Memoirs*, p. 292. Looked at from the revisionist perspectives of Kolko or Williams, with their emphasis on America's ambitions toward economic penetration and financial control, the Treasury's "naïveté" takes on a more sinister cast—the naïveté of a monstrously self-centered child rather than that of a well-meaning innocent.

16. There was, to be sure, a considerable anti-Russian underground, even under Roosevelt, which began to emerge into daylight after the accession of Truman. For an account of early American thinking on using atomic power to extract concessions from the Russians, see Alperovitz, *Atomic Diplomacy*.

Coral Bell disparages the popular notion that America followed a policy of virtuous self-restraint in not pressing its nuclear advantage. The margin never seemed that great. See her *Negotiation From Strength*, p. 29.

17. Much has been made of the seemingly boundless promise of the Truman Doctrine. See, for example, Halle, *The Cold War as History*, pp. 159–60; and Richard Barnet and Marcus Raskin, *After Twenty Years* (New York, 1967), p. 14. Efforts on the part of Kennan and the Policy Planning Staff to introduce qualifications were only marginally successful. See Brown, *The Faces of Power*, pp. 41–45.

18. According to Coral Bell, the West's bargaining power was greatest from early 1952 until mid-1953, when Russia successfully tested her H-Bomb. During this period, the American home base was still virtually invulnerable. NATO's military goals were impressive and European forces rapidly increasing; Greece and Turkey had just joined the Alliance; the European Defense Community was still a possibility; and American force levels were still at their post-Korean peak. *Negotiation from Strength*, pp. 214–15. Ulam believes Bell overstates, although he believes Russia's fear of a militarized West Germany was probably most acute between 1950 and 1954, and they would have paid a fairly high price to avoid it. Ulam, *Expansion and Coexistence*, pp. 506ff.

19. Halle, *The Cold War as History*, p. xiii.

20. Brown, *The Faces of Power*, p. 10.

Chapter IV

1. For the argument that Russia perceived in U.S. policy in Korea a virtual invitation to attack, see André Fontaine, *History of the Cold War* (New York, 1968), vol. 2, pp. 9–31. See also Dean Acheson, *Present at the Creation*, p. 357. See also chap. III, note 12; chap. II, note 1.

2. For an excellent account of American policy and perspectives throughout this period, see Bell, *Negotiation from Strength*.

3. For an account of NATO's early history, see Lord Ismay (Hastings Lionel Ismay, first baron of Wormington), *NATO: the First Five Years* (Paris, 1954).

4. See Adam Ulam, *Expansion and Coexistence*, pp. 559–60; and Andrzej Korbonski, "The Warsaw Pact," *International Conciliation* (May 1969).

5. Harry S. Truman, *Memoirs* (New York, 1966), vol. 2, p. 243; Viscount Montgomery, *Memoirs* (London, 1958), pp. 506–29; and Beaufre, *NATO and Europe*, pp. 20–28. For de Gaulle's early criticisms, see chap. IV, note 8.

6. See my *Britain's Future* (New York, 1968), pp. 41–48; and F. S. Northedge, *British Foreign Policy* (London, 1962), pp. 171–75.

7. For Britain's tepid views toward European integration see the works cited in note 6, above; and Miriam Camps, *Britain and the European Community 1955–1963* (Princeton, N.J., 1964).

8. De Gaulle criticized NATO as early as November 1949, for imposing too excessive American control in return for an inadequate guarantee. Press conference, November 14, 1949; and interview with U.P. representative M. Bradford, July 10, 1950 (microfilm, Bibliothèque de Fondation Nationale des Sciences Politiques).

At the same time, of course, the French government and major French spokesmen, such as Schuman and Bonnet, were among NATO's most active supporters.

9. For the early evolution of postwar German socialist thought, see Hans Edgar Jahn, *Für und gegen den Wehrbeitrag* (Cologne, 1957). For Adenauer's views toward the SPD, see his *Memoirs* (Chicago, 1966), especially pp. 114–15, 163–64, 222–30, 308–9, and 326–27.

10. For a discussion of the evolution of the "flexible response" doctrine, see Brown, *The Faces of Power*, pp. 171–97.

11. Remarks of Secretary of Defense McNamara at the commencement exercises, University of Michigan, Ann Arbor, June 16, 1962, Department of Defense News Release no. 980-62. Small independent nuclear forces within the Alliance, McNamara went on to say, were not only superfluous but dangerous, inviting a preemptive strike by the enemy.

12. For a general treatment of proliferation, see Leonard Beaton and John Maddox, *The Spread of Nuclear Weapons* (London, 1962) ; see also my *Britain's Future*, pp. 94–95, 133–35.

13. Growing uneasiness over Berlin, the perceived "missile gap," and the Kennedy administration's desire to end the Cold War led Adenauer to fear that Germany's best interests were not foremost in America's designs. The MLF scheme was brought forth, in large measure, to ameliorate German fears, and to head off any German movement for a nuclear force of her own.

Meanwhile, de Gaulle took advantage of German-American tension to offer France as the new champion of German interests. (See pp. 67–70, above.) For a discussion of this period, see F. Roy Willis, *France, Germany and the New Europe, 1945–1967* (New York, 1968), pp. 273–331 ; and C. R. Planck, *The Changing Status of German Reunification in Western Diplomacy, 1955–1966* (Baltimore, 1967).

14. For a general theoretical analysis of the possibilities of a European security system, see Pierre Hassner, "Change and Security in Europe," (Adelphi Papers, no. 49; London, 1968), part II. Centre d'Etudes de Politique Etrangère, "Modèles de Securité Européene," *Politique Etrangère*, no. 6, (1967), pp. 519–41. See also

Z. Brzezinski, *Alternative to Partition* (New York, 1965), and "The Framework of East-West Reconciliation," *Foreign Affairs*, January 1968, pp. 256–75.

For differing views on the prospects for European security, see Timothy W. Stanley, *A Conference on European Security*, The Atlantic Council of the United States (Washington, D.C., 1970) and Ivor Richards, "A European Defense Policy," Institute for Strategic Studies, *Survival*, March 1970, pp. 75–80.

Chapter V

1. Charles de Gaulle, *Unity* (New York, 1967), p. 172.
2. *Ibid.*, p. 88.
3. *Ibid.*, pp. 270–71.
4. Charles de Gaulle, *Vers l'Armée de Metier* (Paris, 1944), p. 88.
5. For a general account of postwar Franco-American difficulties, see Edgar Furniss, *France, Troubled Ally: De Gaulle's Heritage and Prospects* (New York, 1960); Alfred Grosser, *La IVe République et sa Politique Extérieure* (Paris, 1961).
6. Charles de Gaulle, *Call to Honor* (New York, 1967), p. 269. For a discussion of former Franco-Russian alliances, see Sir Denis Brogan, *The Development of Modern France* (London, 1967), pp. 316–18, 396–99. For de Gaulle's early efforts to reestablish the Franco-Russian alliance; "which, though repeatedly betrayed and repudiated, remained no less a part of the natural order of things, as much in relation to the German menace as to the endeavors of Anglo-American hegemony," see Charles de Gaulle, *Salvation* (New York, 1967), p. 728.
7. For an individual, objective, and powerful analysis of the arguments for small nuclear deterrents, see General André Beaufre, *Introduction to Strategy* (New York, 1965). For official statements of the Gaullist strategy, see General Pierre Gallois, "Réflexions sur l'Evolution des Doctrines Americaines," *Revue de Défense Nationale* (July 1964); and, General Charles Ailleret, "Opinion sur la Théorie Stratégique de la 'Flexible Response,'" *Revue de Défense Nationale* (August-September 1964). See also Charles de Gaulle, Press Conference (July 23, 1964).
8. For a summary of postwar U.S. strategy, see Brown, *The Faces of Power*; and William W. Kaufmann, *The McNamara Strategy* (New York, 1964).
9. The only "objective" basis for an international monetary system, in de Gaulle's view, was gold. "Yes, gold, which does not

change in nature, which can be made either into bars, ingots or coins, which has no nationality, which is considered, in all places and at all times, the immutable and fiduciary value *par excellence.* Furthermore, . . . it is a fact that even today no currency has any value except by direct or indirect relation to gold, real or supposed. Doubtless, no one would think of dictating to any country how to manage its domestic affairs. But the supreme law, the golden rule— and indeed it is pertinent to say it—that must be enforced and honored again in international economic relations, is the duty to balance, from one monetary area to another, by effective inflows and outflows of gold, the balance of payments resulting from their exchanges." De Gaulle, press conference, February 4, 1965.

10. For a lengthy treatment of de Gaulle's broad political philosophy, particularly as it relates to the future organization of Europe, see my *Europe's Future: The Grand Alternatives* (New York, 1965), chap. 4.

11. For a detailed discussion of de Gaulle's objections to British entry into the EEC, see my *Britain's Future*, chap. 4.

12. For a good summary of postwar Franco-German diplomacy, see Willis, *France, Germany and the New Europe* (New York, 1968).

13. See Adenauer, *Memoirs*, chaps. 2, 13, and 14.

14. The notion of replacing alliance confrontation with a "security system" has been popular in revisionist circles. See, for example, Fritz Erler, former SPD vice-chairman, "The Struggle for German Reunification," *Foreign Affairs*, April 1956, pp. 380–93.

15. Fourteenth Press Conference, October 28, 1966.

16. See Georges Pompidou, radio and television broadcast, December 15, 1969.

Chapter VI

1. According to McNamara, NATO military investments in France were $750 million, of which the U.S. share was $300 million. Unilateral U.S. installations were an additional $550 million. Moving costs of 70,000 American citizens and 820,000 tons of material were about $150 million, with $40 million to $50 million in foreign exchange. U.S., Congress, House, Committee on Foreign Affairs, *Hearings on the Foreign Assistance Act of 1967* (Washington, D.C., April 11, 1967), pp. 132–33 and 140. In 1968 France agreed to 88 million francs for the Council's building and 65 million francs for the material left behind (*Le Monde*, March 2 and 9, 1968), and permitted continuing peacetime use of 390 miles of pipelines (*New*

York Times, March 23, 1967). As the expulsion was officially defined as an opportunity for "streamlining" NATO's command structure and logistic system, the extent and cost of replacement is unclear. See also E. Stein and D. Carreau, "Law and Peaceful Change in a Subsystem: 'Withdrawal' of France from the North Atlantic Treaty Organization," *American Journal of International Law*, July 1968; and K. Hunt, "NATO Without France: The Military Implications" (Adelphi Papers, no. 32, London, December 1966).

2. For differing views on further coordination, see, for example, Timothy W. Stanley, *NATO in Transition* (New York, 1965), chap. 8; Alastair Buchan, *NATO in the 1960s* (New York, 1963), chap. 7; André Beaufre, *NATO and Europe*, chap 7; and Franz Josef Strauss, *Challenge and Response* (New York, 1970), chap. 10. President Johnson suggested NATO consultations for "the full range of joint concerns—from East-West relations to crisis management." *Department of State Bulletin*, October 24, 1966, p. 623; Mr. Nixon's initiatives resulted in the "NATO Committee on the Challenges of Modern Society." See *Department of State Bulletin*, April 28, 1969, p. 354; November 17, 1969, p. 416; and December 29, 1969, p. 624. See also chap. VI, note 3, below, on the Harmel Exercise.

3. Mr. Harmel was the Belgian foreign minister. Studies of détente and reunification, disarmament and arms control, military problems at NATO's southeastern flank, and NATO's relations to conflicts beyond the treaty's area led to a report on the "Future Tasks of the Alliance," published by the Council in December 1967. See *Department of State Bulletin*, January 8, 1968, pp. 49–52. For the initiating Council communiqué of December 1966, see *Department of State Bulletin*, January 9, 1967, p. 49.

4. For de Gaulle's 1958 proposals for a three-power directorate and the U.S. response, see David Schoenbrun, *The Three Lives of Charles de Gaulle* (New York, 1966), pp. 298–99.

5. See, for example, Anatole Shub, *The New Russian Tragedy* (Washington, D.C., 1969).

6. The latest American-German offset agreement, concluded on July 9, 1969, for fiscal years 1970 and 1971, took place at a time when the Germans were still resisting all pressure to revalue and the United States thus had a certain advantage. According to a joint statement, $1.52 billion in foreign exchange was to flow to the United States—$925 million from procurement of U.S. goods and services (61 percent of the total agreement) and $595 million through financial measures (39 percent of the total).

Details were as follows, in millions of dollars:

Military procurement in the United States	800
FRG loan to the U.S. (repayable after 10 years)	250
Purchase by FRG of loans held in portfolio of Eximbank and of outstanding Marshall Plan loans	118.75
Civil procurement in the U.S. by FRG	125
Creation of fund in U.S. by FRG to encourage German investment in U.S.	150
Advance transfers by the FRG for debt repayment to the U.S.	48.75
Retention in the U.S. of interest earned by the FRG on U.S. Treasury deposits	82.50
Total	1,520.00

See *Department of State Bulletin*, August 4, 1969, p. 92.

7. The United States was careful not to oppose or seem opposed to German *Ostpolitik*. In response to rumors of American displeasure, Under-Secretary of State Rostow declared that West Germany "has embarked on a new and promising diplomacy of peace in Eastern Europe, which we strongly support." *Department of State Bulletin*, October 2, 1967, p. 428. In 1968 Rostow sounded the same theme: "Our ally, the Federal Republic of Germany, has embarked upon an Eastern policy designed to rebuild its ties of trade, of culture, and of political relationships to Eastern Europe. If such a policy offers little prospect for the immediate reunification of Germany, it should prepare the way by altering the atmosphere and breaking down the sense of sullen isolation that breeds unreasonable fear. Eventually, in a changed climate, it should not be beyond the realm of possibility that the same inventiveness which has been devoted to building the new environment of Western Europe and of the Atlantic community may find a formula to end artificial barriers that can only be sustained by force. We understand and agree with the new German policy toward the East. We admire the skill and courage of Chancellor Kiesinger and Foreign Minister Brandt. The initiative is properly theirs and we wish it every success." *Department of State Bulletin*, May 27, 1968, pp. 682–83. Secretary of State Rogers has reaffirmed that position. See *New York Times*, Dec. 6, 1969; and the NATO declaration of December 5, 1969, *Department of State Bulletin*, December 29, 1969, pp. 628–30.

8. As against gold reserves of slightly more than $11 billion in late 1969, the United States had incurred net external liquid liabilities of $33.7 billion. For figures on the U.S. balance of payments and international monetary position, see Tables 2 and 3 in the appendix.

9. Private capital inflow to the U.S. fluctuated from $3.4 billion in 1967 to $8.6 billion in 1968, and back to $3.0 billion in 1969.
The figure of $7.1 billion represents the "liquidity balance." The U.S. has two ways of measuring its balance of payments, the official reserves transactions basis and the liquidity basis. The two often yield contradictory results, as indeed they did in 1969. Both take account of changes in official reserve assets, e.g., gold, IMF, etc. The official reserves transactions basis also includes changes in liquid and non-liquid liabilities, but only to *official* foreign holders, i.e., central banks. The liquidity basis, however, also takes account of liquid liabilities to *private* foreign holders (but not liquid assets held by Americans). Measured by the transactions system, our position showed a surplus in both 1968 and 1969. Measured by the liquidity system, it showed a dramatic deterioration to a large deficit in 1969.
Either system may be criticized as misleading. The reserves transactions balance does not take note of the large dollar holdings of private foreigners—balances which could, under certain circumstances, be transferred to foreign central banks and become a claim on U.S. reserves. The liquidity balance, on the other hand, accounts for many U.S. private short-term liabilities, but ignores corresponding U.S. short-term assets. For a discussion see *The Economic Report of the President, 1970* (Washington, 1970), pp. 126–27.

10. In this view, it is in the world's interest to immunize the United States from any balance-of-payments pressures whatsoever, a position which occasionally surfaces in the works of Charles P. Kindleberger. See his "Euro-Dollar and United States Monetary Policy," Banca Nazionale del Lavoro, *Quarterly Review*, March 1969, pp. 3–15.

11. Figures in the text are from *Survey of Current Business*, June 1968, p. 29, and *Economic Report of the President*, February 1970, p. 277. For further figures for other years see Tables 2 and 3 in the appendix. All these statistics are subject to interminable ambiguities, qualifications and refinements. In our figures the transfer of goods under direct military grants is excluded. The degree to which general military sales depend upon America's foreign military presence is more difficult to gauge. Similarly with the consequences of overseas investments for U.S. exports and repatriated earnings in the future. Foreign economic aid introduces many of the same difficulties.
For U.S. defense spending overseas, see chap. VI, note 23. For U.S. private capital overseas, see David T. Devlin and Frederick Cutler, "The International Investment Position of the United States: Developments in 1968," *Survey of Current Business*, October 1969, pp. 23–36. For U.S. aid and capital grants, see OECD, *Development Assistance, 1968 Review* (Paris, 1968).

12. De Gaulle has been the major critic of America's monetary, as well as of her political, hegemony. See his Eleventh Press Conference, February 4, 1965. He is said to have been closely advised on monetary matters by the distinguished monetary economist, Jacques Rueff, one of the leading proponents of increasing the price of gold to establish sufficient new liquidity to banish national currencies from their reserve role. See Jacques Rueff, *Balance of Payments* (New York, 1967); also, his essay in *Monetary Reform and the Price of Gold,* ed. Randall Hinshaw (Baltimore, 1967), pp. 37–46. On the question of American direct investments in Europe, see Jean-Jacques Servan-Schreiber, *The American Challenge* (New York, 1967). For a general study of many of the problems raised by the "integration" of the European and American economies, see Richard N. Cooper, *The Economics of Interdependence* (New York, 1968).

13. The original IMF quota and voting arrangements of 1945 gave the United States and Britain a near majority and the present EEC countries a relatively small role, doubtless reflecting the political and economic realities of the time. But in the machinery for creating Special Drawing Rights, the Six, as the world's major creditors, are given a collective veto. New SDR creation requires 85 percent of the total votes and the Six presently have 16.9 percent.

14. The European Summit Conference at the Hague, December 1 and 2, 1969, with strong French initiative, urged greater monetary cooperation among EEC members. Shortly thereafter, the Six established a $1 billion pool of short-term (three-month) credits, with provisions made for an equivalent second-stage enlargement. *New York Times*, January 27, 1970. Subsequent national and commission plans call for a European Monetary Union within five to ten years. See *New York Times*, February 25, 1970; and *The Washington Post*, February 25, 1970.

15. The source of funds for the Eurodollar market is a subject of much speculation. According to the 1970 *Economic Report of the President*, European central banks were the major source of Eurodollars (p. 128). Milton Friedman, on the other hand, argues that the foreign central bank dollar holdings—some $5 billion from 1964–68—are not enough to account for the size of the Eurodollar market, estimated to be from $30 billion to $40 billion in 1969. Most of the credit, according to Friedman, is created "by a bookkeeper's pen." Dollar claims held by banks in Europe are used, in the normal banking practice, to create a credit pyramid. See "The Euro-Dollar Market: Some First Principles," *Morgan Guaranty Survey*, October 1969, pp. 4–14. For a contrary view, see Fred H. Klopstock, "Money Creation in the Euro-Dollar Market—A Note

on Professor Friedman's Views," *Federal Reserve Bank of New York, Monthly Review*, January 1970, pp. 12–15.

16. In 1969 much of the discrepancy between the official reserves transactions balance (+ $2.8 billion) and the liquidity balance (−$7.1 billion) could be traced to the Eurodollar market. The official transactions balance "improved," not because the United States acquired more foreign exchange, but because several foreign central banks placed their dollars in the Eurodollar market to take advantage of the high interest rates. Their dollar holdings were thus no longer counted as U.S. liabilities in the official transactions balance. Hence the improvement in that balance.

On the other hand, much of the deterioration in the liquidity balance represented a circular flow. American-owned (or based) dollars went to Europe for the high interest rates and were then loaned back to U.S. borrowers. Hence, the liabilities of U.S. banks to their foreign branches grew from approximately $1 billion in 1964 to more than $14 billion in 1969. In the liquidity balance, these liabilities are counted, but not the corresponding private U.S. assets in the Eurodollar market. Hence the decline in our liquidity balance. For the disparity in size between these flows and the total credit pool of the Eurodollar market, see chap. VI, note 15, above. For U.S. balance-of-payments accounting, see Table 2 in the appendix. For a discussion of the impact of the Eurodollar market on the balance of payments, see Jane Sneddon Little, "The Euro-dollar Market: Its Nature and Impact," *New England Economic Review*, May–June 1969, pp. 18–21.

17. See John E. Nash, "U.K. Policy and International Monetary Reform," in Harry G. Johnson and John E. Nash, *U.K. and Floating Exchanges*, Institute of Economic Affairs, Hobart Papers 46 (London 1967), p. 59; and Paul Einzig, *The Euro-Dollar System* (London, 1967), pp. 138–51.

18. See chap. VI, note 13, above.

19. This, with many qualifications, is Friedman's view: "My own conjecture—which is based on much too little evidence for me to have much confidence in it—is that demand is raised less than supply and hence that the growth of the Euro-dollar market has on the whole made our balance-of-payments problem more difficult." "The Euro-Dollar Market: Some First Principles," p. 11. Fred H. Klopstock of the Federal Reserve Bank of New York agrees with Friedman's conclusions, if not his methodology. See his "Money Creation in the Euro-Dollar Market," pp. 12–15.

20. See Congressman Henry S. Reuss, chairman of the International Exchange and Payments Subcommittee of the Joint Economic Committee, in February 1967, as cited in *The Banker*, March 1967. For a further discussion of these ideas, see my *Britain's Future*, pp. 119–28.

21. See McCloy, *The Atlantic Alliance*, p. 48.

22. See Robert Skidelsky, *Politicians and the Slump* (London, 1967), chap. 1 and *passim*.

23. The total negative balance-of-payments impact of U.S. defense spending abroad for fiscal year 1969 was a record $4.8 billion as compared to $4.53 billion in 1968. 1968 figures (in millions of dollars) broken down by region, reveal 1,533 spent in Western Europe and the remainder as follows: Canada, 285; Latin America, 105; Japan, 581; Korea, 301; Philippines, 169; Ryukyu Islands, 202; Thailand, 318; and Vietnam, 558. For sources and general discussion, see Cora E. Shepler and Leonard G. Campbell, "United States Defense Expenditures Abroad," *Survey of Current Business*, December 1969, pp. 40–47.

24. Professor Raymond Vernon, a leading authority on international business, thinks it possible that advanced countries might sign a treaty limiting the capacity of overseas subsidiaries to interfere with foreign national policies. While Vernon believed the United States might not initiate such a move, it would probably be amenable to a European intiative. See *New York Times*, January 14, 1970.

Chapter VII

1. De Gaulle, *Unity*, p. 269.

2. It is in the tradition of Richelieu and Talleyrand, not of Napoleon, and the *Ancien Régime*, not the empire, that de Gaulle generally saw himself. The true genius of France, de Gaulle believes, lies in her vocation for precision, balance, and measure, which was most aptly expressed in the *Ancien Régime* at its best. See his *La France et son Armée* (Paris, 1938), pp. 47 and 63–72.

Americans are not notably addicted to *mesure*, and therein, from de Gaulle's point of view, lies the great argument.

3. Prominent revisionist historians who point up the American share in the Cold War include William A. Williams and Gabriel Kolko, who stress the militant economic imperialism of the United States, or Louis J. Halle and Adam Ulam, who stress the mutual incomprehension of such radically different social and political systems. George Kennan occasionally touches on the federalist theme developed here, as, of course, does de Gaulle in his *Complete War Memoirs* (New York, 1967). It is also a major theme for Richard Barnet and Marcus Raskin as well as Stanley Hoffmann, Ronald Steel, and others.

4. See Eugene V. Rostow, *Law, Power and the Pursuit of Peace*, chaps. 1–3.

As for Wilson, some historians tend to downplay his image as isolationist and utopian, picturing him instead as an economic liberal of conventional plumage, ready to intervene externally to ensure a favorable economic position for the United States. See Williams, *The Tragedy of American Diplomacy*, pp. 53–83.

Others, at least, see a certain tension between Wilson's rhetoric and his actions. The utopian belief that evil could be rooted out once and for all did not reinforce isolationism. Instead, it led Wilson to become "the most extraordinary interventionist in Latin America in the history of the United States." Arthur Link, *Wilson, the Struggle for Neutrality* (Princeton, N.J., 1960), p. 495. A figure more sensitive to human failings might have been more inclined to leave his neighbors alone.

5. A paraphrase of de Gaulle on interdependence, *Vers l'Armée de Métier*, p. 88.

6. Such was Kennan's description of the language of the Vandenberg Resolution. *Memoirs* (Boston, 1967), p. 409. See also p. 25, above.

7. For a powerful and learned exposition of this view, see Rostow, *Law, Power and the Pursuit of Peace*. The basis for a world rule of law, he argues, is not to be found in the utopian announcements of the United Nations charter, which, "like the precedents of Nurenberg, are new roots in an old forest" (p. 15), but in the "prudent rule of reciprocal safety" (p. 43) embodied in our network of regional defensive alliances: "In every perspective, regional coalitions of free nations built around American nuclear power remain the indispensable base and precondition of world peace (p. 50). Of these, the strongest and most important is the North Atlantic Treaty, manifesting a relationship which is "rich in the complexity of deep and intimate human ties" (p. 91).

In fairness to the former Under-Secretary of State for Political Affairs, it should be said that he, almost alone among high American officials—at least until the arrival of Ambassador Shriver in Paris—made strenuous efforts to compose Franco-American differences in the Alliance and hence to transform the factual hegemony into the ideal concert. His partial success, reflected in the Harmel Exercise, illustrated not only his own personal gifts, but also the fundamental limitations on transatlantic consensus. For a discussion of the Harmel Exercise, see chap. VI.

8. For a more extended discussion of these matters, see my *Coleridge and the Idea of the Modern State* (New Haven, Conn., 1966), chap. 9. See also my *Europe's Future*, chap. 1.

9. For a theoretical statement of the role of indifference in diplomacy and hence an important qualification on the "field of force" view of international politics, see Arnold Wolfers, "The Pole of Power and the Pole of Indifference," *Discord and Collaboration: Essays on International Politics* (Baltimore, 1962), pp. 81–102.

10. Stanley Hoffmann, *Gulliver's Troubles*, p. 278.

Chapter VIII

1. Experts are still divided about the effect of the Czech invasion on the military balance in Europe. The strengthening of supply and communication lines and the addition of some 55,000 Russian troops in Central Europe must be weighed against the resistance of the Czech population and the decreased political reliability of the Czech army. Statements by former SACEUR General Lyman L. Lemnitzer and British Defense Secretary Denis Healey in press conferences on February 1, 1969, suggested an official view that the military balance in Central Europe had not been altered by the Czech invasion. See *New York Times*, February 2, 1969.

2. In judging comparative mobilization times, distance is only one among several important factors. Others would include the degree of combat-readiness at home and the degree of infrastructure support already available at the front. With the new advances in troop transportation, American soldiers in a state of combat alert could theoretically be in Europe in a matter of hours, or in a few days if sea transport were used. But would the mobilization system be activated in time? For example, NATO, with full knowledge of extraordinary Warsaw Pact activity prior to the Czech invasion, could have chosen to undertake a corresponding mobilization in the West, but did not. Theoretically, the massed Warsaw Pact troops might have invaded West Germany instead. But, given the size of western forces, any build-up adequate for an invasion of the West would necessarily be much larger and slower and even less possible to conceal. (The return of American troops during such a build-up might, in itself, be an impressive contribution to deterrence.) In so massive a mobilization and countermobilization, the risk of escalation to nuclear war is sufficiently plausible to make so old-fashioned a scenario seem highly unreal. With all parties possessing nuclear arms, it is difficult to see what conceivable aims would justify such terrible risks. If Europe had only token conventional forces, the situation might be different, but this is far from the case. See also chap. II, notes 17 and 18.

3. See, for example, Stanley, *NATO in Transition*, p. 387.

4. For the military doctrine behind such deterrents, see chap. V, note 7, above. For a study of the costs of various types of nuclear forces, see Leonard Beaton, "Capabilities of Non-Nuclear Powers," *A World of Nuclear Powers*, ed. Alastair Buchan (Englewood Cliffs, N.J., 1966), pp. 13–38. Beaton assumed the French capable of building "a small force of Super-Power quality." For a good analysis of the French nuclear force, see Wilfrid L. Kohl, "The French Nuclear Deterrent," *The "Atlantic Community" Reappraised*, ed. Robert H. Connery (New York, 1968).

5. The treaty prohibits the transfer of actual nuclear weapons and nuclear explosive devices or control over them to any recipient, but prohibits assistance in manufacturing or otherwise acquiring such weapons only to nonnuclear states (Article I). The question of succession to nuclear status is not dealt with in the treaty. Secretary of State Rusk explained the American view on this matter before the Senate Committee on Foreign Relations on July 10, 1968, stating that the NPT "would not bar succession by a new federated European state to the nuclear status of one of its former components." U.S., Congress, Senate, *Hearings on the Nonproliferation Treaty*, July 10, 11, 12, and 17, 1968, pp. 5–6. The Soviets strongly oppose any arrangements that might appear to lead to an independent nuclear force for the FRG or even greater influence in a collective force. Their displeasure would doubtless dampen German ambitions for a controlling role in any Anglo-French nuclear force, at least as long as the Russians are conciliatory in the East.

6. See Alastair Buchan, *Stability in Europe* (London, 1963), pp. 201–12, and *Europe's Future, Europe's Choices* (London, 1969), pp. 99–101; or Franz Josef Strauss, *The Grand Design* (New York, 1966), pp. 54–57, and *Challenge and Response* (New York, 1970), p. 156.

7. See Robert S. McNamara's testimony before the House Armed Services Committee, January 30, 1963.

8. Former Secretary of State Rusk very occasionally sounded as if the United States were clearly willing to accept and promote changes in NATO's structure along these lines: ". . . we would welcome now, as before, a European caucus, if they want to call it that, in NATO, something like a European defense community, as a full partner in a reconstituted alliance." See *Department of State Bulletin*, December 25, 1967, p. 858.

9. The Great Coalition abandoned the traditional aversion toward direct contacts with high-ranking eastern officials and sought to promote better conditions in Germany as a whole through a policy of "small steps." The concept of special, so-called *"inter se* relations" began to evolve, relations somewhat comparable, it was sometimes said, to the special relations within the British Commonwealth during the 1930s and 1940s. Brandt coined the term *"geregeltes Nebeneinander"* (i.e., regulated side-by-side) for these special relations. See, for example, U. Scheuner, "Entwicklungslinien der deutschen Frage," in *Europa Archiv*, July 10, 1969, pp. 453–65.

Chapter IX

1. A noteworthy exception is Roger Masters, *The Nation is Burdened* (New York, 1967). See also my *Europe's Future,* chap. 6.

BIBLIOGRAPHY

Acheson, Dean. *Present at the Creation*. New York, 1969.

Adenauer, Konrad. *Memoirs*. Chicago, 1966.

Ailleret, Charles. "Opinion sur la Théorie Stratégique de la 'Flexible Response,' " *Revue de Défense Nationale*, August–September 1964.

Alperovitz, Gar. *Atomic Diplomacy*. New York, 1965.

Aron, Raymond. *Peace and War*. New York, 1968.

Ball, George W. *The Discipline of Power*. Boston, 1968.

Barnet, Richard, and Raskin, Marcus. *After Twenty Years*. New York, 1967.

Beaton, Leonard, and Maddox, J. *The Spread of Nuclear Weapons*. London, 1962.

Beaufre, André. *Introduction to Strategy*. New York, 1965.

———. *NATO and Europe*. New York, 1966.

Bell, Coral. *Negotiation From Strength*. New York, 1963.

Brown, Seyom. *The Faces of Power*. New York, 1968.

Brzezinski, Z. "The Framework of East-West Reconciliation," *Foreign Affairs*, January 1968.

Buchan, Alastair. *Arms and Stability in Europe*. London, 1963.

———. *Europe's Future, Europe's Choices*. London, 1969.

———. *The Future of NATO*. Carnegie Endowment for International Peace, 1967.

———. *NATO in the 1960s*. New York, 1963.

———. "The United States as a Global Power," *International Journal*, Canadian Institute of International Affairs, Spring 1969.

———. (ed.) *A World of Nuclear Powers*. Englewood Cliffs, N.J., 1966.

Bundy, W. McGeorge. *The Pattern of Responsibility*. Boston, 1952.

Calleo, David P. *Britain's Future*. New York, 1968.

———. *Coleridge and the Idea of the Modern State*. New Haven, Conn., 1966.

———. *Europe's Future: The Grand Alternatives*. New York, 1965.

Camps, Miriam. *Britain and the European Community 1955–1963.* Princeton, N.J., 1964.

Centre d'Etudes de Politique Etrangères. "Modèles de Sécurité Européenne," *Politique Etrangère,* no. 6 (1967).

Cleveland, Harlan. "NATO After the Invasion," *Foreign Affairs,* January 1969.

———. "The Resurrection of NATO," *Foreign Service Journal,* April 1968.

Connery, Robert H. (ed.). *The "Atlantic Community" Reappraised.* New York, 1968.

Cooper, John Sherman. *Report to the Military Committee of the North Atlantic Assembly.* Fall 1969. (*mimeo.*)

Cooper, Richard N. *The Economics of Interdependence.* New York, 1968.

Cottrell, Alvin J., and Dougherty, James E. *The Atlantic Alliance, A Short Political Guide.* London, 1964.

Council of Economic Advisors. *Economic Report of the President, 1970.* Washington, D.C., 1970.

De Gaulle, Charles. *Complete War Memoirs.* New York, 1967.

———. *La France et Son Armée.* Paris, 1938.

Djilas, Milovan. *Conversations With Stalin.* New York, 1962.

Einzig, Paul. *The Euro-Dollar System.* London, 1967.

Enthoven, Alain C., and Smith, K. Wayne. "What Forces for NATO and From Whom?" *Foreign Affairs,* October 1969.

Fontaine, André. *History of the Cold War.* New York, 1968.

Friedman, Milton. "The Euro-Dollar Market: Some First Principles," *Morgan Guaranty Survey,* October 1969.

Furniss, Edgar. *France, Troubled Ally: De Gaulle's Heritage and Prospects.* New York, 1960.

Gallois, Pierre. "Réflexions sur l'Evolution des Doctrines Americaines," *Revue de Défense Nationale,* July 1964.

Graebner, Norman A. *Cold War Diplomacy.* Princeton, N.J., 1962.

Grosser, Alfred. *La IVe République et sa Politique Extérieure.* Paris, 1961.

Halle, Louis J. *The Cold War as History.* New York, 1967.

Healey, Denis. "NATO, Britain, and Soviet Military Policy," *Orbis,* Spring 1969.

Heath, Edward. "Realism in British Foreign Policy," *Foreign Affairs,* October 1969.

Hinshaw, Randall (ed.). *Monetary Reform and the Price of Gold*. Baltimore, 1967.

Hoffmann, Stanley. *Gulliver's Troubles*. New York, 1968.

Houthakker, H. S., and Stephen P. Magee. "Income and Price Elasticities in World Trade," *The Review of Economics and Statistics*, May 1969.

Hunt, K. "NATO Without France: The Military Implications." (Adelphi Papers, no. 32.) London, December 1966.

International Monetary Fund. *Direction of Trade*. Monthly.

―――. *International Financial Statistics*. Monthly.

Institute for Strategic Studies. *The Military Balance, 1969–1970*. London, 1969.

Johnstone, Allen W. *United States Direct Investment in France*. Cambridge, Mass., 1965.

Kennan, George F. *Memoirs*. Boston, 1967.

Kindleberger, Charles P. "The Euro-Dollar and the Internationalization of the United States Monetary Policy," Banca Nazionale del Lavoro, *Quarterly Review*, March 1969.

Kolko, Gabriel. *The Politics of War*. New York, 1968.

Lerner, Daniel, and Aron, Raymond. *France Defeats EDC*. New York, 1957.

Liddel-Hart, Sir Basil. *The Revolution in Warfare*. New Haven, Conn., 1947.

Liska, George. *Europe Ascendant*. Baltimore, 1964.

―――. *War and Order: Reflections on Vietnam and History*. Baltimore, 1968.

Little, Jane Sneddon. "The Euro-dollar Market: Its Nature and Impact," *New England Economic Review*, May-June 1969.

McCloy, John. *The Atlantic Alliance: Its Origins and Its Future*. New York, 1969.

McNamara, Robert S. Statement. *The Fiscal Year 1969–73 Defense Program and the 1969 Defense Budget*. Washington, D.C., 1968.

―――. *Statement Before the Senate Armed Services Committee on the Fiscal Year 1969–73 Defense Program and 1969 Defense Budget*. Prepared January 22, 1968.

NATO Information Service. *NATO—Facts and Figures*. Brussels, 1969.

Northedge, F. S. *British Foreign Policy*. London, 1962.

Office of the Assistant Secretary of Defense, Systems Analysis.

Evaluation of NATO and Pact Conventional Forces in Central Europe. October 1968.

Organization for Economic Co-operation and Development. *Economic Outlook.* Quarterly.

———. *Main Economic Indicators.* Monthly.

Planck, Charles R. *The Changing Status of German Reunification in Western Diplomacy 1955–1966.* Baltimore, 1967.

Report of the Congressional Conference on the Military Budget and National Priorities. June 1, 1969. (*mimeo.*)

Rueff, Jacques. *Balance of Payments.* New York, 1967.

Schellenger, Harold Kent, Jr. *The S.P.D. in the Bonn Republic: A Socialist Party Modernizes.* The Hague, 1968.

Schlesinger, Arthur, Jr. "Origins of the Cold War," *Foreign Affairs*, October 1967.

Shub, Anatole. *The New Russian Tragedy.* Washington, 1969.

Shulman, Marshal D. "Sowjetische Vorschläge für eine europäische Sicherheitskonferenz (1966–1969)," *Europa Archiv*, October 10, 1969, pp. 671–84.

Skidelsky, Robert. *Politicians and the Slump.* London, 1967.

Stanley, Timothy W. *NATO in Transition: The Future of the Atlantic Alliance.* New York, 1965.

———. "A Strategic Doctrine for NATO in the 1970's," *Orbis*, Spring 1969.

Steel, Ronald. *Pax Americana.* New York, 1967.

Strange, Susan. "The Sterling Problem and the Six," Chatham House, *European Services* (London), no. 4 (1967).

Strauss, Franz Josef. *Challenge and Response: A Program for Europe.* New York, 1970.

———. *The Grand Design.* New York, 1966.

Triffin, Robert. *The World Money Maze.* New Haven, Conn., 1966.

Truman, Harry S. *Memoirs.* New York, 1966.

Ulam, Adam. *Expansion and Co-Existence.* New York, 1968.

U.S., Congress, House, Committee on Foreign Affairs. *Hearings, The Mutual Security Program.* June 1951.

———, House, Special Subcommittee on National Defense Posture of the Committee on Armed Services. *Review of a Systems Analysis Evaluation of NATO vs. Warsaw Pact Conventional Forces.* September 1968.

———, Joint Economic Committee Subcommittee on Economy

in the Government. *Hearings, The Military Budget and National Economic Priorities.* 1969. Part I.

————, Senate, Committee on Appropriations. *Hearings, Department of Defense Appropriations.* December 8, 1969.

U.S. Department of Commerce, *Survey of Current Business.* Monthly.

Waltz, Kenneth. "Stability in a Bi-Polar World," *Daedalus,* Summer 1964.

Williams, William A. *The Tragedy of American Diplomacy.* New York, 1961.

Willis, F. Roy. *France, Germany and the New Europe, 1945–1967.* New York, 1968.

Wolfers, Arnold (ed.). *Discord and Collaboration: Essays on International Politics.* Baltimore, 1962.

INDEX

Acheson, Dean, 24, 25, 151, 152
Adenauer, Konrad, 52, 57, 160; foreign policy of, 61, 67–68, 134. *See also* Germany
AFCENT, 34
Africa, French role in, 72–73
AFSOUTH, 30
Agricultural policy, EEC, 96
Ailleret, General Charles, 159
Air forces: NATO's tactical, 31–32; Western European, 125
Algeria, 49
Alliances: Franco-American, 62; Franco-German, 71; Franco-Russian, 61–62; imperial nature of, 13; U.S.-Western European, 71; Western, 122; Western dissolution of, 106
Alliluyeva, Svetlana, 39n
Alperovitz, Gar, 155, 156
American political imagination, 107, 117–18
Anglo-French nuclear force, 169
Antiballistic missiles (ABMs), 9; against China, 143
Arendt, Hannah, 13
Aron, Raymond, 150
Atlantic Alliance. *See* North Atlantic Treaty Organization
Atlantic community: decline of, 46–53, 70, 76; defensive nature of, 43; European coalition in, 64; myth of, 61, 121; origins of, 124–27; and world rule of law, 109–10
Atlanticism: as ideology of U.S. hegemony, 78, 100; revival of, 81–82; supported by German socialists, 83

Balance of payments: and Eurodollar market, 165; European, 31; U.S., 84–88, 91, 94–95, 163

Balance of power: American interpretation of, 105; in Asia, 22; European, 53; and federalism, 104; and isolationism, 106
Balance of terror, 4
Balance of trade. *See* Trade
Barnet, Richard, 157, 166
Beaton, Leonard, 144, 158, 168
Beaufre, General André, 152, 157, 159, 161; on NATO, 27, 28n
Bell, Coral, 151, 156, 157
Benelux, 127
Blocs: De Gaulle's campaign against, 65, 67; preservation of, 106; unrest within, 5–6
Brandt, Willy: eastern policy of, 137; opposition to German neutralism, 134. *See also* Germany
Britain: and de Gaulle, 66; and EEC, 133; as Europe's natural leader, 48; and independent nuclear force, 51, 78, 127; resistance to U.S. hegemony, 50–51; special relation with U.S., 48, 61. *See also* Military manpower; Nuclear forces
British empire, 13–16
Brogan, Sir Denis, 159
Brown, Seyom, 44, 151, 156, 157, 158, 159
Brussels Pact (1948), 48, 152
Brzezinski, Zbigniew, 159
Buchan, Alastair, 144, 150, 152, 161, 168, 169
Bucharest Foreign Ministers' Conference (1966), 130
Budapest Foreign Ministers' Conference (1969), 130
Bundy, W. McGeorge, 151, 152
Bureau of the Budget, 120
Bureaucracy: growth of, 17; insulation of, 117–18; in NATO,

175